TRANSPORTATION ISSUES, POLICIES AND R&D

HEAD RESTRAINTS AND WHIPLASH:

THE PAST, PRESENT AND FUTURE

TRANSPORTATION ISSUES, POLICIES AND R&D

Additional books in this series can be found on Nova's website at:

https://www.novapublishers.com/catalog/index.php?cPath=23_29&seriesp=Transportation+Issues%2C+Policies+and+R%26D

Additional e-books in this series can be found on Nova's website at:

https://www.novapublishers.com/catalog/index.php?cPath=23_29&seriespe=Transportation+Issues%2C+Policies+and+R%26D

TRANSPORTATION ISSUES, POLICIES AND R&D

HEAD RESTRAINTS AND WHIPLASH:

THE PAST, PRESENT AND FUTURE

EDIRIWEERA DESAPRIYA

Nova Science Publishers, Inc.
New York

For permission to use material from this book please contact us:
Telephone 631-231-7269; Fax 631-231-8175
Web Site: http://www.novapublishers.com

LIBRARY OF CONGRESS CATALOGING-IN-PUBLICATION DATA

Head restraints and whiplash : the past, present, and future / Ediriweera Desapriya and others.
p. ; cm.
Includes bibliographical references and index.
ISBN 978-1-61668-150-0 (softcover)
1. Whiplash injuries. 2. Automobiles--Occupant restraint systems. I. Desapriya, Ediriweera.
[DNLM: 1. Whiplash Injuries--prevention & control. 2. Automobiles--standards. 3. Head Protective Devices--standards. 4. Head Protective Devices--trends. 5. Public Policy. 6. Risk Factors. WE 725 H432 2010]
RD533.5.H43 2010
617.5'3044--dc22

2009052733

Published by Nova Science Publishers, Inc. ✦ New York

CONTENTS

Preface		**vii**
Introduction		**ix**
Chapter 1	Scientific Literature: The Relationship between Head Restraints and Whiplash	**1**
Chapter 2	Risk Factors for Whiplash Injury and Associated Disorders	**13**
Chapter 3	Knowledge and Awareness of Correct Head Restraint Positioning	**25**
Chapter 4	Evolution of Changes in Regulations, Standards, and Policy for Head Restraints	**33**
Chapter 5	Strategies to Reduce Whiplash Injuries and Future Directions	**41**
Conclusion		**61**
Acknowledgments		**63**
References		**65**
Index		**85**

PREFACE

While fatalities due to rear impacts are lower than in other collision types, injuries represent a much larger percentage (approx. 26% of all injuries) and typically occur as neck strain (e.g. whiplash). Whiplash injuries occur when the sudden movement between the head and torso results in injuries to the soft tissues of the neck. This mainly occurs in rear-end collisions. The effectiveness of vehicle seats has been tested over the last 35 years and previous research shows that head restraints could reduce injuries by 14 to 18%. Vehicle seats have seen an evolution in terms of their characteristics and design since the 1970s from bucket seats to yielding seats to high retention seats, and more recently, energy absorbing anti-whiplash seats. Anti-whiplash seats were developed to absorb as much energy as possible while reducing the occupant acceleration and minimizing the movements of the neck. Other restraints that have been tested to be effective are active head restraints and restraints with better static geometry. Research shows that serious neck injuries arising primarily from low impact rear-end motor vehicle collisions can be effectively prevented by the use and proper adjustment of head restraints with better geometry.

In 2008, the World Congress on Neck Pain highlighted that PREVENTION IS POSSIBLE, concluding that it was possible to reduce the risk of serious neck injuries arising from motor vehicle collisions by 35% if people purchased vehicles with good head restraints and adjusted them appropriately. This book provides: 1) a review of the history, evolution, and scientific literature surrounding head restraints and whiplash-related injury; 2) the risk factors, and prevalence of inappropriate use of head restraints 3) the need to educate drivers, occupants, fleet owners, and policy-makers concerning the importance of head restraints that have obtained a rating of "good" or higher and the efficacy of the proper adjustment of head restraints for prevention of serious neck injuries; 4) new strategies addressing the three Es of injury prevention including education, engineering, and enforcement, with a particular focus on social marketing and occupational health strategies that increase proper head restraint adjustment for preventing whiplash-related injuries and associated impairments and disability. Gaps in the literature and future directions surrounding the prevention of neck injury and whiplash are also provided.

The ultimate objective for the book is to be a useful tool to increase awareness around the importance of the use and the proper adjustment of highly rated head restraints according to scientific evidence, highlight the benefits of various prevention strategies and discuss future directions in neck injury and whiplash prevention.

INTRODUCTION

Unintentional injuries, particularly road traffic injuries, are a key component of the burden of non-communicable diseases. Traffic-related injuries account for a substantial share of the disease burden in many countries worldwide. It is predicted that traffic collisions will become the 3rd major cause of mortality by 2020 (Murray, 2006). Reducing the severity of injuries from traffic collisions is one of the most effective means of improving traffic safety. In order to reduce the number of people killed and/or injured in traffic collisions, many research studies have identified the risk factors that can significantly influence traffic-related injuries and fatalities. Researchers have demonstrated the efficacy of interventions that could significantly reduce traffic-related collisions (Subzwari et al., 2008). Rear-end collisions are the most common type of traffic collision and whiplash is the most common complaint of those claiming bodily injury (Cassidy et al., 2000; Spitzer et al., 1995).

THE ISSUE

In recent years, many countries have seen a significant increase in neck injuries arising from motor vehicle collisions, commonly known as 'whiplash-related injuries'. Previous research shows that serious neck injuries arising primarily from low impact rear-end motor vehicle collisions can be effectively prevented by the use and proper adjustment of highly-rated head restraints in motor vehicles (Farmer et al., 2003). Given that rear-end collisions will occur, the severity of whiplash-related injuries are dependent on three predominate factors: 1) the crashworthiness performance offered by the vehicle and its seating/safety system, 2) the ability of the seating/safety system to properly adjust to the occupant's characteristics (i.e. size, weight, age, gender, etc.), and 3) whether the occupant and seating/safety system are properly positioned or activated at the time of the collision. At present, improved seat and head restraint design technology in some vehicles offer greater protection to mitigate whiplash-related injuries, however due to a lack of knowledge resulting in a poor selection of vehicle features, and/or a lack of proper adjustment by the occupant, the effectiveness of these design improvements to reduce the overall societal cost of whiplash-related injuries has been severely limited.

A major issue in whiplash prevention is the lack of proper adjustment of the seating safety system by the occupant (or responsible driver) for proper protection. In manual systems (e.g. seat belts, child safety seats, head restraints, etc.), proper use requires sufficient knowledge and participation by the responsible occupant and remains a significant challenge to overcome, and one that may never be fully achieved. This factor alone contributes heavily to the lack of effectiveness of head restraints where manual adjustment is required for proper performance.

To allow significant advancement in reducing whiplash-related injuries and associated impairments: 1) a larger proportion of vehicles with enhanced seating system performance in preventing whiplash are required in a changing vehicle fleet, and 2) the seating system in each vehicle must be properly adjusted and operated to suit the seated occupant in order to optimize the whiplash prevention capabilities of that system.

These issues are not new, but rather are a continuing barrier to achieving improved success in reducing the whiplash-related injuries and associated impairments and disability.

The major aims of this book are to: 1) review the history, evolution, and scientific literature surrounding head restraints and whiplash-related injury; 2) educate the drivers, occupants, fleet owners, and policy-makers concerning the need to purchase vehicles with head restraints that have obtained a rating of "good" or higher and the efficacy of the proper adjustment of head restraints for prevention of serious neck injuries; and 3) propose new strategies based on injury prevention theory and methods. The three Es of injury prevention including education, engineering, and enforcement, will be addressed, with a particular focus on social marketing and occupational health strategies to increase awareness and change behaviors surrounding proper adjustment of head restraints for preventing whiplash-related injuries and associated impairments and disability. A discussion of future directions surrounding the prevention of neck injury and whiplash will be provided.

A Brief History of Whiplash Injury

With the development and use of railways in the 19th century, whiplash-like injuries were first noted following train collisions. Formerly called "railroad spine", patients most often reported severe emotional disturbance leading them to be categorized as psychoneurotic (Scaer, 2007). With the invention of the motor vehicle, the first reports of persisting neck pain following motor vehicle collisions were found as early as 1919 (Scaer, 2007). American surgeon Harold Crowe coined the term "whiplash" in 1928 in the medical literature. He highlighted the issues related to neck movement to describe the sudden jolting of the head and neck in vehicle crashes (Croft et al., 2002; Farmer et al., 1999; Kullgren et al., 2000; Richter et al., 2000). In 1953, Gay and Abbott reviewed the cases of 50 patients who suffered whiplash injury over a 4 year period. The symptoms they described included pain, limitation of neck movement, spasm and tenderness in the cervical spinal musculature, with associated symptoms in the upper thoracic spine and shoulder girdle. Following Harold Crowe's work (1928), Gay and Abbott were among the first to suggest the concept of whiplash in the early 1950s. The word "whiplash" was in the title of Gay and Abbott's article (1953) and they later described the related symptoms that followed after rear-end collision impacts, introducing the medical term "whiplash injury".

Following a survey of 100 patients who had been referred for neurosurgical consultation on cervical whiplash injury, Gotten (1956) reported that after settlement of claims, approximately 30% of all traffic collisions resulted in whiplash-type neck distortions. This was the second article published in the Journal of the American Medical Association (JAMA) in a 3 year period that discussed the topic of whiplash injuries. Gotten (1956) noted "a wide divergence among specialists as to the severity of the injury" (p 866) and commented that "psychoneurotic symptoms were so prevalent and seemed to be such a dominant factor" (p 866) in these patients (Galasko et al., 1993; Richter et al., 2000).

In 1995, the Québec Task Force (QTF) on Whiplash-Associated Disorders (WAD) published the first best-evidence synthesis and consensus report on whiplash as a supplement to the journal, SPINE. The scientific committee found 10,382 published articles on whiplash (1980-April 1994) and only 1,204 met the preliminary screening criteria. Following a more rigorous review, there were only a core group of 294 studies with sufficient relevance and scientific merit for in-depth review and only 62 of the 294 (21%) were considered high enough quality to inform best practices. Although there was insufficient research to make strong evidence-based guidelines, the QTF laid the groundwork for future research and recommended a classification system relevant to clinicians and researchers.

Early Definitions of Whiplash

Whiplash is commonly defined by the lay person to denote any injury to the neck sustained in a road traffic collision. Further, it implies that the neck behaves as a 'whip', that is, a low-velocity, high-energy input at the base producing a high-velocity excursion at the tip. The use of slow-motion video-recording of volunteers and dummies has shown the biomechanical forces at play in rear-end collisions. In 1964, McNab defined whiplash as 'acceleration extension injury'. However, as Morris (1989) noted 'acceleration hyperextension injury' would be a more appropriate term.

The terms "whiplash" and "whiplash associated disorders" (WAD) are used to describe neck disorders related to sudden movement of the neck. Whiplash is considered an injury to the soft tissue of the cervical spine, caused by the sudden acceleration of the head relative to the torso. This typically occurs during a rear-end collision, mostly at low impact velocities, typically less than 20 km/h (Deng, 1999; Deng et al., 2000a; Howard et al., 1998), and includes an acceleration-deceleration mechanism of energy transfer (Spitzer et al., 1995). Characteristic symptoms of WAD include neck pain, headache, and arm tingling. Whiplash injuries sustained in motor vehicle collisions have become an issue of growing concern. It is important to note that these types of injuries occur due to other mechanisms as well, not simply motor vehicle collisions (Jakobsson et al., 2004a; Kullgren et al., 2000; Minton et al., 2000). This book focuses on whiplash injuries and WAD that are related to motor vehicle collisions, primarily rear-end collisions.

Transition of the Term Whiplash Injury to "Whiplash Associated Disorders" (WAD)

Over time, the concept and definition of whiplash has evolved from "whiplash injury" to WAD recognizing the complex biopsychosocial factors that impact the clinical manifestation of symptoms following a motor vehicle collision. WAD partly replaced the older term "whiplash injuries" following the QTF's report published in 1995 (Spitzer et al., 1995). The new term 'WAD' encompasses a group of complaints characterized by a variety of symptoms such as pain and stiffness in the neck that often lacks any external or radiological evidence (Spitzer et al., 1995). The pathology accounting for whiplash symptoms has been and continues to be, the subject of considerable medical interest, investigation and debate.

More recently, many researchers have dropped the term "whiplash" and replaced it with the phrase "neck pain and associated disorders, arising from motor vehicle collisions", for several reasons. Firstly, "whiplash" incorrectly describes the real biomechanical process of changes in the occupant's head and torso motion during a rear-end collision. Secondly, the high prevalence of neck pain in the general population, in workers and after motor vehicle collisions - twelve month prevalence estimates of neck pain are 30-50%, (Hogg-Johnson et al., 2008), a broader conceptual framework is needed to consider a more extensive range of biopsychosocial factors that influence the natural course of history of neck pain in these populations. However, for the purpose of this book when we refer to "whiplash-related injuries" we are referring to neck injuries and the associated disorders as well as the "perceived" and real impairments, and disability.

A major and obvious outcome of whiplash or WAD is neck pain. In a best-evidence synthesis (1980-2006), to better understand the burden and determinants of neck pain due to WAD after traffic collisions, researchers found that the incidence of WAD has increased in western countries over the past 30 years and is likely to be at 300 per 100,000 inhabitants in North America and western Europe (Holm et al., 2008). Personal, societal, and environmental factors are of importance, although the evidence of determinants for WAD is quite meager. Attendance at the emergency department for WAD after a traffic collision has also increased over time, although this may reflect an increase in public awareness for seeking care. In terms of seeking care or filing an insurance claim, it appears that younger people, those with prior neck pain and females were at higher risk (Holm et al., 2008). There is preliminary evidence for the efficacy of whiplash protection devices such as properly positioned head restraints that limit head extension in rear-end collisions (Holm et al., 2008). Insurance claim data has indicated that active head restraints and adjustable head restraints rated as "good", were associated with a reduction in insurance claims for WAD, and had a greater effect among female drivers. Interestingly, researchers found no evidence to support the notion that crash severity was related to WAD (Holm et al., 2008).

MECHANISM OF WHIPLASH INJURY OCCURRENCE

Whiplash injuries and the mechanism that results from rear-end collisions are not fully understood. Biomechanical research has shown that the neck experiences compression, tension, shear force, flexion, and extension at different stages and at varying levels of the neck (Deng et al., 2000a). Compression of the neck occurs when the thoracic spine straightens and results in an upward ramping of the torso on the seat (Deng et al., 2000a). The upward motion of the torso combined with the static head, results in a compressed neck, followed by tension. Extension occurs in the lower end of the neck, while the upper neck is in flexion, causing an s-shape (Deng et al., 2000a). The different biomechanical processes that the neck undergoes contribute to stretching of the facet capsular ligaments, causing pain (Deng et al., 2000a).

However, over the last few decades, effective countermeasures for whiplash injuries have been recognized (Buitenhuis et al., 2009; Schmitt et al., 2003). Numerous vehicle collision studies and occupant injury studies indicate that low-speed rear impacts can lead to neck and back injuries causing long-term disability and discomfort. Although these injuries are usually classified as having a low threat to life, they are often associated with large societal costs (Gibson and McIntosh, 1997; Kahane, 1982; Spitzer et al., 1995; Viano and Olsen, 2001). It is evident that design changes to seat systems and/or head restraints to improve their use and the occupant protection they offer could make a positive impact in mitigating injuries from rear-end impacts.

Whiplash - Minor Injury and Low Priority?

Most whiplash injuries are regarded as minor (1) using the Abbreviated Injury Scale (AIS), and as such, are treated as low priority by most road safety organizations and vehicle manufacturers (Ardoino, 1996; Maher, 2000). However, contrary to these findings, research conducted in many countries (Baddick and Love, 1990; Kahane, 1982; Livingston, 1992; 1993; Maher, 2000; Nygren, 1984; O'Neill et al., 1972; O'Neill, 2000; Spitzer et al., 1995; Verhagen et al., 2007a; Viano and Olsen, 2001; Young et al., 2005) reported that insurance claim frequency was highest in rear impact collisions and whiplash injuries.

The cost of long-term whiplash injuries to front-seated occupants in the United Kingdom (UK) was estimated to be approximately £3 billion annually (Hynd et al., 2008). Hopkin and Simpson (1995) demonstrated that whiplash is by far the most costly injury, involving 31% of the total cost though it accounted for only a little over 15% of all injuries in the UK. Whiplash injuries appeared in 36% of all claims to the New South Wales Motor Collisions Scheme (Gibson and McIntosh, 1997). In Quebec, Canada, the 5,000 whiplash cases each year account for 20% of all traffic injury insurance claims (Spitzer et al., 1995). On average, whiplash injury costs Quebec $18 million annually (Spitzer et al., 1995). Sixty-eight percent of motor vehicle collision claims in British Columbia, and 85% in

Saskatchewan, were related to whiplash injuries (Spitzer et al., 1995). In the US, the estimated annual cost of whiplash injury is $8.2 billion (Edwards et al., 2005) and $1.2 billion in the UK (Avery et al., 2007). Whiplash injuries account for more than half of the automobile insurance claims in Japan (Huang and Huston, 2003). It is important to note that whiplash injuries resulting from rear impacts have one of the highest rates of long-term injury-related consequences (Hell and Langwieder, 1998).

Whiplash injuries also account for a large proportion of annual costs in terms of medical care and income support. An Australian study presents evidence showing that the incidence of whiplash has increased in recent decades and that in South Australia, approximately 4,000 claims for whiplash at a cost of $50 million are made annually, for a population of 1.5 million (Osti et al., 2005). The total annual cost of whiplash injuries due to rear impacts in the US, which includes economic costs as well as costs related to a reduced quality of life, has been estimated at approximately $2.7 billion (Haneline, 2009). In addition, chronic whiplash associated disorders (WAD) are associated with issues related to social functioning, daily anxiety and satisfaction with different aspects of life (Sterner and Gerdle, 2004).

Relationship of Head Restraints and Whiplash Injuries

For the last 40 years, vehicle safety researchers have been acquiring information on the ability of head restraints to mitigate injuries resulting from rear-end collisions. Severy and colleagues (1968) produced a clear description of the ability of good seat design and head restraint positioning, to prevent potentially injurious head-neck kinematics in rear-end collisions. They concluded that well designed safety seats would protect most passengers against sustaining any rear-end collision injuries (Severy et al., 1968). They showed that head restraints in rear-end collisions were as important as seat belts in frontal collisions. The primary method of preventing whiplash-induced injury in motor vehicles is the correct adjustment and proper use of a head restraint. A properly adjusted head restraint will help to protect against whiplash, and the potential for long-term injury (Deng et al., 2000b).

Padded head restraints have been used since the mid 1950s. They were also proposed as countermeasures to the hyperextension phase of whiplash (Ruedemann, 1957). In the 1960s, head restraint and whiplash injury research informed federal mandates for vehicle head restraints (Severy et al., 1968). As a result of the research, Federal Motor Vehicle Safety Standard (FMVSS) 202 required that all passenger cars manufactured for sale in the US after December 31, 1968 included head restraints in the front outboard seating positions. The installation of head restraints in the front seats of Australian vehicles has also been compulsory since 1972 under Australian Design Rule (ADR) 22. The early research recommended that making head restraints compulsory in rear seats was not justified because of the small number of neck injuries that occurred in rear seated occupants (Maher, 2000). This is not the case today.

DEFINITIONS FOR HEAD RESTRAINTS

The US Insurance Institute for Highway Safety (IIHS) has created definitions for various types of head restraints. The definitions are presented in Table 1.

Table 1. Definitions for various types of head restraints

Head restraint "Head restraint means a device designed to limit the rearward displacement of an adult occupant's head in relation to the torso in order to reduce the risk of injury to the cervical vertebrae in the event of a rear impact" (p. 1).
Integrated head restraint "Integrated head restraint or fixed head restraint means a head restraint formed by the upper part of the seat back, or a head restraint that is not height adjustable and cannot be detached from the seat or the vehicle structure except by the use of tools or following the partial or total removal of the seat furnishings" (p. 1).
Adjustable head restraint "Adjustable head restraint means a head restraint that is capable of being positioned to fit the morphology of the seated occupant. The device may permit horizontal displacement, known as tilt adjustment, and/or vertical displacement, known as height adjustment" (p. 1).
Active head restraint "Active head restraint means a device designed to automatically improve head restraint geometry during an impact" (p. 1).
Automatically adjusting head restraint "Automatically adjusting head restraint means a head restraint that automatically adjusts the position of the head restraint when the seat position is adjusted" (p. 1).

Source: The Insurance Institute for Highway Safety (IIHS, 2008, p.1).

Why Head Restraints Are Required

In a rear-end collision the differential movement of the head and torso can be limited by either a high seat back or a separate head restraint positioned behind and close to an occupant's head (States et al., 1972). As part of recognition of this intervention in mitigating injuries, front-seat head restraints have been required in all new cars sold in many countries, including Canada, since 1969. Ruedemann (1969) reported on the introduction of a new device in motor vehicle design - the head restraint, introduced to prevent whiplash injury in rear-end collisions. However, it's unfortunate to note that nearly 40 years after introducing head restraints, whiplash injury from rear-end collisions remains an important public health problem with a significant economic and health burden (O'Neill, 2000; Welcher and Szabo, 2001), and despite the continuing innovation in head restraint design, whiplash injury claims in rear-end collisions have continued to increase worldwide (Viano and Olson, 2001).

Rear-End Collisions and Cost of Whiplash Injuries

Quinlan and colleagues (2004) noted that rear-end collisions continue to be a major cause of long-lasting neck and back injuries (i.e. whiplash) and a significant cause for pain and suffering (Quinlan et al., 2004). These injuries also constitute an enormous societal cost due to the following key components:

1. High and extended medical expenses
2. Time away from the workplace
3. Numerous liability and insurance claims

According to NHTSA (2001), an average of 805,581 whiplash injuries occurs annually, that cost the US $5.2 billion (NHTSA, 2001). Whiplash injury claims are documented to have increased over the past two decades in Canada, with the societal costs exceeding $464 million per year in the province of British Columbia alone (Kumar et al., 2000). Whiplash injuries represent 68% of vehicle injury claims in British Columbia (Kumar et al., 2000). However, the main limitations of these cost estimates were that they did not attempt to incorporate the costs associated with the reduction in the quality of life of the whiplash sufferers; which may in part be due to methodological difficulties in quantifying changes in quality of life following this type of injury. Estimates in the UK indicated that the cost of long-term whiplash injuries to front-seated occupants was approximately £3 billion annually. The same report highlighted that a static geometric head restraint requirement is the first step in mitigating low-speed rear impact injuries (Hynd et al., 2008).

Effectiveness of Head Restraints in Reducing Rear Impact Whiplash Injuries

As previously stated, the primary function of head restraints is to minimize the relative rearward movement of the head and neck in rear impacts (Maher, 2000). Frontal impact rebound protection has been highlighted as the secondary function of head restraints (Maher, 2000). Effectiveness of head restraints subsequent to FMVSS 202 has ranged from 13% to 18% reduction in injuries (Maher, 2000). It is reported that the neck injury incidence rate was 29% in vehicles without head restraints as compared to 24% in head restraint-equipped vehicles (O'Neill et al., 1972).

States and colleagues (1973) interviewed 439 Rochester, New York drivers and right-front passengers of rear-struck vehicles during the first three months of 1972. Results indicated that a total of 43% of occupants in vehicles without head restraints reported neck injuries, compared to 37% in vehicles with head restraints. Texas collision data analyzed in 1972, 1974 and 1977, compared rear-impact driver injury rates for cars of model year 1968 with those of model year 1969 (Kahane, 1982). After analyzing more than 20,000 drivers in each group, researchers found that 7.6% of those in the 1968 model were injured compared with 7% in the 1969 models (Kahane, 1982). After adjusting for the fact that 12% of 1968 models had head restraints and 12% of 1969 models did not, the effectiveness of head restraints was estimated to result in a 13% reduction in injuries, including 17% for fixed head restraints and 10% for adjustable head restraints (Kahane, 1982).

Incorrect Adjustment of Head Restraints and Risk of Whiplash Injury

Previous research has indicated an increased risk for neck injury in rear-end impacts if the head restraints are incorrectly positioned. There is an increased risk for neck injury in rear-end impacts if the backset is large, and/or the head restraint is low (Baddick and Love, 1990; Chapline et al., 2000; Farmer et al., 1999; Jakobsson, 2005; Kahane, 1982; Livingston, 1993; Nygren, 1984; O'Neill, 2000; O'Neill et al., 1972; Olsson et al., 1990; Young et al., 2005). This information was vital in setting the background for the geometric tests of seats and head restraints conducted by car manufacturers and safety organizations such as the IIHS. The purpose of correctly adjusted head restraint positioning is to ensure proximity between the head and the head restraint. The ideal head restraint position occurs when there is zero backset and the top of the head is level with the top of the head restraint (Chapline et al., 2000, Nygren, 1984; O'Neill, 2000).

Following implementation of the US head restraint requirements, research has shown a decrease in neck injury rates for rear-end collisions (Kahane, 1982; O'Neill et al., 1972; States and Balcerak, 1973). O'Neill and colleagues (1972) reported that the incidence of neck injury (sample of 5663 rear-end collisions) was 5% less in head restraint-equipped vehicles compared to those without. Similarly, States and Balcerak (1973) noted a 14% reduction of whiplash injuries in vehicles equipped with head restraints.

After reviewing a random sample of 5,000 rear-end collision claims, Farmer and colleagues (1999) noted that head restraints must have good geometric design to prevent whiplash injuries (Farmer et al., 1999). Additional research indicated that properly positioned head restraints (i.e. no lower than the head's center of gravity and no farther behind the head than 11 cm) were more effective in preventing neck pain following rear impact (Chapline et al., 2000). In exploring sex differences, results were statistically significant for women, yet the effectiveness of the head restraint in reducing neck pain was similar for both sexes (42% and 44% reduction in risk of pain, respectively) (Chapline et al., 2000). Researchers reported that there were too few male participants with correctly positioned head restraints to allow adequate statistical power; therefore results for men were not significant (Chapline et al., 2000).

Definition for Correct Adjustment of Head Restraints

To prevent soft-tissue neck injuries through the correct adjustment and use of head restraints, specific recommendations were provided. The height of a restraint and the gap between the head and the restraint are critical in influencing injury risk. Head restraints in all sitting positions and minimum restraint height should correspond to the top of the head of at least the 50th percentile of seated adult males. Ideally, restraint height should correspond to the top of the head of the 95th percentile of seated adult males. The smallest distance possible should be left between the back of the head and the point where it would first meet the restraint (Farmer et al., 1999; Fockler et al., 1998; Viano and Gargan, 1995).

Adjustable head restraints were defined as correctly adjusted if the top of the head restraint was approximately level with the top of the driver's ears or higher. Therefore, in Fockler's study (1998) all head restraints observed to be positioned so that the top was lower than the driver's ears were defined as incorrectly adjusted (Fockler et al., 1998). Head restraints were rated as poor if, in the lowest position, they were more than 10 cm below the top of the head or 12 cm or more behind the head and in the highest position, were more than 8 cm below the top of the head or 10 cm or more behind the head (Cullen et al., 1996).

Chapline and colleagues (2000) noted that US regulations mandated a minimum height of 27.5 inches above the seating reference point for head restraints in the highest position, however, there are no regulations governing a minimum height in the lowest position. In addition, a majority of the current US vehicle fleet has adjustable head restraints yet most individuals do not correctly adjust them (Chapline et al., 2000). They also suggested that the use of European head restraint standards would greatly benefit North American women and certainly men, however, until then, proper adjustment of head restraints should be encouraged (Chapline et al., 2000).

Research indicates that during normal driving, if all adjustable head restraints were adjusted to the correct vertical height, then a reduction of 28.3% in whiplash injuries and a significant reduction in the incidence of soft tissue injuries, from rear-end collisions can be expected (Chapline et al., 2000; Viano and Gargan, 1995).

Chapter 1

SCIENTIFIC LITERATURE: THE RELATIONSHIP BETWEEN HEAD RESTRAINTS AND WHIPLASH

This section will provide a review of the scientific literature surrounding the relationship among vehicle stiffness, head restraints and whiplash. The literature includes research that utilizes dummies, computer simulations, cadavers and human volunteers, as well as comparison studies.

Over time, investigations were conducted using Hybrid II dummies, Hybrid III dummies, the Rear Impact Dummy (RID/RID2) necks, Biofidelic Rear Impact Dummies (BioRID), de Jager MADYMO necks, Whiplash Artificial Cervical Spine (WACSY) necks, Post-Mortem Human Subjects (PMHS; cadavers), volunteers, and car occupants in real rear-end impacts.

Human volunteers have been used in staged, slow speed, rear-end impacts for over 50 years to test the kinematics of the motion of the volunteer, head and seat acceleration (DeRosia and Yoganandan, 2000). This research began in the 1950s (Severy et al., 1955), initiating additional research and awareness concerning seatback stiffness, head restraints, torso ramping, preparedness of the volunteer, the effects of pre-activated muscles on head motion and the potential for injuries (DeRosia and Yoganandan, 2000). Severy and colleagues (1955; 1968) were the first to assess the effects of head restraints through the use of dummies who were subjected to rear impacts. This early work lead to the establishment of head restraint standards in the US (FMVSS 202) and the recognition of head restraints as a safety device. In the 1960s Mertz and Patrick (1967) began utilizing sled simulators and testing car-to-car impacts with humans, dummies, and human cadavers. They examined muscle activation, effects of head restraints and seatback stiffness using electronic and photographic sensors. In the early 1970s researchers began investigating forward impacts and the effects on humans (DeRosia and Yoganandan, 2000). From the 1970s to the early 1990s, very little scientific research was conducted concerning human volunteers and slow speed, rear-end impacts. Research re-emerged in the 1990s and was pursued assertively from that point forward (DeRosia and Yoganandan, 2000).

HEAD-TO-NECK KINEMATICS

Cervical hyper-extension was the most popular hypothesized mechanism for injury in the early research. Flexion of the cervical spine, shear load, localized cervical compression and tension, spinal canal pressure gradients, and muscle strain were all additional mechanisms for injury that were tested extensively (Szabo, 2000).

Darok and colleagues (2000a) applied computer simulations using the occupant simulation software MADYMO to investigate the Neck Injury Criterion (NIC) (Darok et al., 2000a). Additional research testing the shear force hypothesis of whiplash injury was conducted using computer simulations in combination with a high-speed x-ray system (Deng et al., 2000a). The research demonstrated the complex kinematics of the neck during rear-end impact showing that the neck experiences compression, tension, shear force, flexion, and extension at different stages and at varying levels of the neck (Deng et al., 2000a). When the thoracic spine straightens and an upward ramping of the torso on the seat occurs, compression of the neck ensues (Deng et al., 2000a). The upward motion of the torso combined with the stationary nature of the head, results in compression of the neck, followed by tension. The 'head lag' phenomenon also contributes to the tension in the neck (Deng et al., 2000a). This occurs when the torso moves faster than the head in the horizontal direction. The concept of shear force occurs in the neck when the torso moves forward due to an impact from behind. A flexion moment on the whole neck is a result of the shear force impact at the junction of the thoracic and cervical spine (Deng et al., 2000a). The lower end of the neck is then subjected to extension, while the upper neck is in flexion, causing an s-shape to occur (Deng et al., 2000a). The combination of compression, tension, shear force, flexion, and extension contribute to stretching of the facet capsular ligaments (Deng et al., 2000a).

Based on the numerous rear-end motor vehicle collisions that resulted in whiplash injuries and neck pain, research efforts increased and there was a major boost in the development of anthropometric test devices (ATD) and their components (Kim and Prasad, 2000). In the US, researchers from Chalmers University of Technology introduced the rear impact (RID) dummy neck in the early 1990s, which later developed into the BioRID P3. TNO developed the TRID

(TNO Rear Impact Dummy) neck and proceeded to develop an ATD specific to rear impact collisions (RID) (Kim and Prasad, 2000).

Dummies such as the Hybrid III with MADYMO with sophisticated cervical spine models were used to test head restraint properties (Kleinberger et al., 1999). Testing of the Hybrid III dummy indicated that it had adequate biofidelity for determining head-neck kinematics in rear impacts at various test severities (Kim and Prasad, 2000). Interestingly, the Hybrid III and the TRID necks were closer in stiffness to cadavers rather than human volunteers. Research indicated that the Hybrid III could be used to estimate the risk of high severity neck injuries in rear impacts (Kim and Prasad, 2000).

The experience of pain has been investigated over time. McConnell and colleagues (1995) found that middle-aged healthy male subjects exposed to rear impacts of 4-8 kph experienced mild cervical strain without affecting range of motion. The facet capsules have been isolated as the point where whiplash-associated pain is centralized (Bogduk and Marsland, 1988). Upper cervical flexion and lower cervical extension are thought to cause headaches and neck pain (Yoganandan et al., 1998; 1999). Ono and colleagues (1997) showed that compressive loading on the cervical spine results from upward motion of the upper torso, which in turn causes the lower vertebral segments to extend beyond their normal range.

HEAD RESTRAINT HEIGHT

Head-to-neck kinematics is influenced by the seat height, and there are definite benefits to increasing head restraint height (Jakobsson et al., 1993; Kleinberger et al., 1999; Szabo, 2000). Research that specifically investigated the effects of head restraint height on occupant kinematics and WAD is extensive and seems to have progressed from 1985 onwards including the work of: Nygren et al., 1985; Jakobssen et al., 1993; Ono and Kanno, 1993; Viano and Gargan, 1995; Eichberger et al., 1996; Minton et al., 1997; Hell and Langwieder, 1998; Kleinberger et al., 1999; Welcher and Szabo, 1999; Farmer et al., 1999.

Research conducted in the 1990s revealed that while it was better than no head restraint at all, the standard head restraint design was in the incorrect position to prevent injury (McConnell et al., 1993; McConnell et al., 1995). These results motivated future research that sought to update and improve the head restraint. In the mid to late 1990s, researchers investigated slow-speed collisions involving energy absorbing bumper systems (Szabo et al., 1994; Szabo and Welcher, 1996; West et al., 1993) and barrier impacts. West and colleagues

(1993) calculated that a barrier impact speed of 11 kph was the torque threshold past which injuries would occur. Szabo and colleagues (1994; 1996; Welcher and Szabo, 1999) investigated the effects of adding a layer of padding to the head restraints. They found that the muscle did not develop tension until the flexion phase of the impact, whereas with unpadded head restraints the muscles tensed earlier increasing the risk of neck pain (Szabo et al., 1994; Szabo and Welcher, 1996; Welcher and Szabo, 1999). Viano and Gargan (1996) reported that if adjustable head restraints were placed in the up position, the relative risk of whiplash injury would be decreased by 28.3% (Viano and Gargan, 1996).

In 1992, Gane and Pedder developed a head restraint measuring device (HRMD) to help provide an accurate and consistent means of measuring the position of head restraints (Gane and Pedder, 1996). The HRMD measured the vertical height and the setback of the head restraints in the front seats (Gane and Pedder, 1996). Although various factors affect the 'best' position for the head restraint, the HRMD provides a tool to identify those head restraints that are most effective in reducing neck injuries (Gane and Pedder, 1996).

Several studies showed that there was a reduced risk of whiplash injury in rear collisions due to the improvements that were made in head restraint geometry (Chapline et al., 2000; Farmer et al., 1999; 2003). Although, researchers also realized that improvements in geometry alone would not provide adequate protection for neck injuries (Zuby and Lund, 2007). This resulted in improvements to seatback design such as strong seatbacks with cushion systems that allowed an occupant's body to sink (Saab and General Motors), and some manufacturers also included active head restraints (Viano, 2002; Wiklund and Larsson, 1998). These improvements in seat design allowed for better support of the head and less stress on the neck (O'Neill, 2000).

Neck Injury Criterion (NIC)

The Neck Injury Criterion (NIC) is a tool that was commonly used to estimate dangerous impact conditions on the soft tissue injuries of the neck (Bostrom et al., 2000; Darok et al., 2000). Hybrid III dummies were used to investigate the efficacy of the NIC tool. Results indicated that the NIC seemed to represent the amount of kinetic energy loaded to the occupant, such that the correlation between Delta-V and the NIC was striking (Darok et al., 2000). In terms of the crash duration, there was an inverse relationship such that a decrease in NIC occurred with an increase in collision duration (Darok et al., 2000). There were low NIC and neck loads whenever the head restraint was close to the head (horizontal distance), and there was an increase in NIC when the head restraint was lowered (vertical distance). When the head restraint was removed, the neck torque increased dramatically, indicating that the NIC was designed for assessing the retraction motion of the neck and not for predicting hyperextension injuries (Darok et al., 2000). In testing seatback stiffness, results showed a possible reduction of the NIC and neck loads by using a stiff recliner joint. Researchers deduced that contact of the head with the head restraint occurs early and limits the amount of retraction and extension motion (Darok et al., 2000). Overall, the results showed a correlation between the NIC and velocity change, crash pulse, and head restraint position. The NIC was also correlated with the neck extension angle, head angular acceleration and neck torque (Darok et al., 2000). With respect to validation of the NIC, during the human volunteer tests, subjects did not complain about injuries in the cervical spine region after the test, and no neck pain was reported days later (Darok et al., 2000). Results showed that the NIC increases with the horizontal distance between the head and head restraint. In addition, an approximate correlation between the NIC and the maximum relative angle of the head and torso was also observed (Darok et al., 2000).

DELTA-V

Reports indicate that injuries and fatalities in motor vehicle collisions are increasing in tandem with vehicle velocity. Delta-V or the 'change in velocity' is an important factor in the majority of motor vehicle-related injuries and outcomes. However literature shows that unlike other motor vehicle collision-related injuries, whiplash injuries occur even at a Delta-V of 10-15 kph. Therefore, Delta-V has limited value in the prognosis of whiplash injuries.

SEATBACK STIFFNESS

Seatback stiffness is a factor that contributes to the reduction of injury (Szabo, 2000). Mertz and Patrick (1967) were among the first to investigate the effects of seatback stiffness using dummies. They demonstrated decreased neck bending moments for the seat with reduced stiffness (Mertz and Patrick, 1967). Additional researchers replicated the findings indicating that there was decreased acceleration and velocity at the base of the neck, and a reduction in head rotation relative to the torso (Haland et al., 1996; Koch et al., 1995; Svensson et al., 1993; Watanabe et al., 1999).

SEATBACK ENERGY ABSORPTION

An additional variable is the influence of seatback energy absorption (Szabo, 2000). Seatbacks with strong structural cross-members do not allow the occupant to sink into the seat, hindering energy absorption and reducing the space between the head and head restraint (Himmetoglu et al., 2008). Researchers found decreased adoption of the cervical s-curvature with an energy absorbing seat (Dippel et al., 1997), and the overall beneficial effects of increased seat energy absorption (Bostrom et al., 1997; Geigl et al., 1994; Gupta et al., 1996; Kihlberg, 1969; Martinez and Garcia, 1968; Olsson et al., 1990; Parkin et al., 1995; Welcher and Szabo, 1999). Volvo's WHIPS (Whiplash Protection System) seat also incorporates an energy absorbing feature and tests were conducted using BioRID dummies and Hybrid IIIs to examine acceleration and torso acceleration (Jakobssen et al., 1999; Lundell et al., 1998). Toyota's seat (Whiplash Injury Lessening; WIL) system was also successful in reducing several injury-related parameters using the Hybrid III dummy with a TRID II neck, testing rear impacts (Sekizuka, 1998).

Recent research investigating energy-absorbing seat designs included the following "essential design criteria for seats equipped with anti-whiplash features (Himmetoglu et al., 2008, p. 585):

1) Good head restraint geometry in terms of head restraint height and backset
2) Effective crash energy-absorbing characteristics
3) Minimum neck internal motion (OC relative to T1 motion), reduced S-shape (or retraction)
4) Low neck forces (compression, tensile, shear) and moments
5) Reduced ramping
6) Minimum rearward displacement of the seat
7) Limited seatback rebound
8) No activation of anti-whiplash devices during normal use
9) Improved performance at all impact severities"

In addition, results showed that WMS, DWMS, RFWMS, and DRFWMS anti-whiplash seat design concepts all performed well in reducing whiplash, and there was not much contrast among the results (Himmetoglu et al., 2008). However, it was found that the seat design concepts with inner seatback frames were advantageous compared to those without frames (Himmetoglu et al., 2008). Inner seatback frames provide earlier head restraint contact and reduce seatback angle, especially in higher severity impacts (Himmetoglu et al., 2008). In effect, the anti-whiplash seat performs best when it effectively absorbs the collision energy while simultaneously providing early head support (Himmetoglu et al., 2008).

THE ENTIRE SEAT PLAYS A ROLE

Since the head restraint on its own, was not as effective as it could be, researchers deduced that the performance of the entire seat plays a role in reducing the risk of neck injuries. The WHIPS was introduced in Volvo vehicles in 1998 (Jakobsson et al., 2008). The BioRID dummy was used in the WHIPS testing procedures. The three guidelines underpinning the WHIPS were: a) reduce occupant acceleration; b) minimize relative spine movements; and c) minimize the forward rebound into the seat belt (Jakobsson et al., 2000). The innovation of the WHIPS seat consisted of a recliner mechanism, modified backrest characteristics and head restraint geometry (Jakobsson et al., 2008). The seat has been on the market for over 10 years and has proven effective in reducing injury, based on real-world data (Farmer et al., 2003; Kullgren et al., 2007; Jakobsson et al., 2008; Jakobsson and Norin, 2004). Results of the WHIPS showed that for occupants over 14 years of age without prior neck problems and at a moderate impact severity, neck injury reducing effects were 33% for initial neck injuries and 53% for symptoms lasting greater than one year (Jakobsson and Norin, 2004). The effects were more pronounced in women than in men, indicating that the WHIPS may be more effective in reducing the risk of neck injury in women (Jakobsson and Norin, 2004). Testing performed on the WHIPS demonstrated factors such as the importance of occupant characteristics, sitting posture, turned head and increased head to head restraint distance, all increased the risk of neck injury (Jakobsson et al., 2008).

When they examined the effects of seat design, the most comfortable seat was the WHIPS design and relative to the torso, it also exhibited the lowest head center of gravity in rearward translation and the lowest head acceleration in extension and flexion (Welcher and Szabo, 1999). This new generation of yielding seats has proven effective in reducing whiplash (Viano, 2008). The seats feature: perimeter frame seatback; strong frame structure; strong recliners; open seatback; EA pelvic strap; pocketing into seatback; pelvic drop on rear loading; and, high, forward head restraint (Viano, 2008). This seat has evolved over time beginning with a yielding seat in the 1970s, to a stiff seat in the 1990s, and now the use of the current high retention seat. The high retention seat allows for minimal neck displacement when there is an increase in speed. The addition of the active head restraint has made it superior to earlier seat designs.

Active Head Restraints

Active head restraints were introduced because the population was typically not positioning their head restraints appropriately. Active head restraints were designed to actively decrease the distance between the head and head restraint immediately following rear impact acceleration. Active head restraints function by moving the head restraint forward (closer to the head) and upward when the lower unit is loaded by the pelvis, when a rear impact occurs. In the late 1990s, the active head restraint became popular, and tests were conducted using human subjects. Saab created a head restraint that moved forward when pressure was exerted by the upper torso during rear impact (SAHR; Wiklund and Larsson, 1998). This was based on the earlier SAHR (Self Aligning Head Restraint). As summarized above, Volvo's new seat modified the stiffness of the head restraint, upper seatback, lower seatback, and incorporated energy absorption of the seatback (WHIPS; Lundell et al., 1998). Toyota also tested a seat named the Toyota Whiplash Injury Lessening (WIL) system using human subjects (Sekizuka, 1998). The seat had an adjustable head restraint, and a seatback with reduced upper torso stiffness. General Motors also improved their seat designs including improved stiffness and geometry, adjustable head restraints or self-aligning head restraints (Insurance Institute for Highway Safety; IIHS, 1999). Mercedes Benz developed an active head restraint known as the NECK-PRO System. It was introduced in the E- and C-class models beginning in 2005. The active head restraint moves towards the occupant's head to shorten/close the gap between the head restraint and the head in the event of a rear-end collision (Hartlieb et al., 2007). The advantages of the NECK-PRO System include: reduced whiplash by minimizing head to torso motion; whiplash protection yet a comfortable head restraint position; activation at low Delta-V; non-aggressive deployment of the head restraint; activation is independent of occupant mass; easily reversible by the driver (Hartlieb et al., 2007). Mercedes Benz' active head restraint uses an on-board crash sensor that activates a linkage in the head restraint (Motor Insurance Repair Research Centre Thatcham, 2006).

New technology was developed in the UK - the Smart Head Restraint System (Acar et al., 2007). The Smart Head Restraint System proposes to move the head restraint into an optimum position and continuously monitor the changes in the position of the head and make adjustments to ensure that the head restraint is constantly ready for an impact to occur (Acar et al., 2007). This system consists of mechanical horizontal and vertical adjustment mechanisms with sensors to detect and monitor the person's head, and control software that continuously adjusts the head restraint position (Acar et al., 2007). Researchers expect that this system will increase the likelihood of the proper head restraint positioning and correct adjustment to ensure that at the point of impact there will be maximized whiplash protection and a decrease in future economic cost (Acar et al., 2007).

Testing of the active head restraints were conducted on sled tests utilizing the BioRID II dummy, while different pulses (shape and Delta-V) were applied. The tests became part of the consumer ratings and are performed according to the test protocols for IIWPG-Rating (IIHS and Thatcham), EuroNCAP, and FMVSS202a. As an overall summary, the neck shear force (Fx) was reduced by 50% and neck tension force (Fz) by 35%, compared to a passive head restraint. The test results were confirmed in vehicle to vehicle tests. In 2008, researchers investigated the reduction in neck injuries with an active head restraint (Kitagawa et al., 2008). They compared rear-impact simulations using a fixed head restraint and an active head restraint. Tests on the SAHR reduced whiplash injury risks by 75 +/- 11% from an 18 +/- 5% incidence in 85 occupants with standard head restraints to 4 +/- 3% in 92 occupants with SAHR (Viano and Olsen, 2001). Results for the active head restraint indicated a decrease in NIC and joint capsule strain due to the forward and upward motion of the head restraint, following a reduction in the magnitude of shear deformation in the facet joint (Kitagawa et al., 2008). The authors concluded that neck injury could be reduced by supporting the head earlier and through the trajectory stopping joint deformation (Kitagawa et al., 2008).

Overall Seat Design Principles

Viano (2008) provided an overview of design principles and seat characteristics that lower the risk of whiplash. The summary revealed that seat stiffness, frame strength, and a high forward head restraint are important factors in controlling neck displacement (Viano, 2008). The addition of an active head restraint had a greater impact on reducing neck displacement and load (Viano, 2008). Recent research delved more deeply into the biomechanics, kinematics and mechanisms for whiplash-related injuries such as the rate of change of acceleration (Hynes and Dickey, 2008). This work investigated whether the head acceleration response to whiplash-like perturbation profiles was affected by a change in the rate of applied acceleration (termed "jerk") (Hynes and Dickey, 2008). The main findings suggest that when trying to predict injury from whiplash-like perturbations, Delta-V, mean acceleration or peak acceleration should not be the sole factors to consider (Hynes and Dickey, 2008). Jerk should be evaluated independently of acceleration level (Hynes and Dickey, 2008).

VEHICLE SEAT RATINGS

The International Insurance Whiplash Prevention Group (IIWPG) was formed to assist with designing and implementing a low speed rear impact sub-system test to simulate the typical scenario in which whiplash injuries occur (Avery, 2008). The role of the published test results was to contribute pressure on the vehicle manufacturers to improve the seat and head restraint designs. The IIWPG includes international research centers that have testing sites at Thatcham (UK) and the Insurance Institute for Highway Safety (IIHS) (US). Over the past 3 years, test results using 250 new vehicle seats, have been published internationally (Avery, 2008). The first step in the testing is to statistically rate the geometry of the seat. The test consists of a simulated rear collision on a rear acceleration sled device using a BioRID II dummy that represents a 50th percentile male occupant (Avery, 2008). The test simulates a 16 km/hr rear impact to determine a dynamic rating of how well the seat supports the torso, neck and head (Avery, 2008). The main outcome is to limit the retraction of the head relative to the neck, therefore the encouraged design philosophy is of energy absorption at T1 (1st thoracic vertebrae) and early support of the OC (occipital condyle) (Avery, 2008). Through a combination of geometric and dynamic test ratings, the seat is rated as "good", "acceptable", "marginal" or "poor". When researchers compared vehicle model years 2005 to 2007, using European and US seat ratings, results indicated an 81% increase in seats that achieved a "good" rating and a corresponding 44% reduction in those that achieved a "poor" rating (Avery, 2008). These results are encouraging as they show that whiplash injuries can be reduced through independent benchmarking (Avery, 2008).

Over time, the design changes to seatbacks and the role of active head restraints reduced the rates of neck injury claims following rear collisions (Farmer et al., 2003; Jakobsson and Norin, 2004; Viano and Olsen, 2001). Recent research suggests that higher rated seats resulted in fewer neck injuries to the occupants that required 4 or more weeks of medical attention compared with lower rated seats (Kullgren et al., 2007). In addition, more recently, Farmer and colleagues (2008) investigated the relationship of dynamic seat ratings to real-world neck injury rates (Farmer et al., 2008). Results indicated that neck injuries tended to increase as seat ratings decreased, and driver neck injury rates were higher for vehicles with poorly rated seats (Farmer et al., 2008). However, drivers' neck injury rates for vehicles with acceptable or marginal seats did not demonstrate expected results (Farmer et al., 2008). The risk factor of being female was again apparent as female drivers were much more likely to claim neck injuries than male drivers (21.7% vs 13.9%) (Farmer et al., 2008). In terms of long term injuries, neck injury rates lasting 3 months or more, were 35% lower for seats rated good in comparison to poorly rated seats (Farmer et al., 2008).

In 2006, Thatcham investigated the proposed EuroNCAP test procedure on 93 seats. A modified SAE J826 H-point manikin, combined with a head restraint measuring device (Gane and Pedder, 1996; 1999), and the BioRID II dummy were used to test the parameters (Avery et al., 2007). Results showed that a seat that achieved a high score from the proposed EuroNCAP system was likely to achieve a good rating with the IIWPG criteria. The compatibility of the rating systems was recognized and reinforced the quality of the seats.

COMPARING DUMMIES TO HUMANS

More recent research has compared dummies to human subjects on several parameters (Jonsson et al., 2008). Researchers compared stature, weight and backset of the BioRID II (Biofidelic Rear Impact Dummy; Schneider, 1983) to the same variables on seated volunteers in a car (Jonsson et al., 2008). Results showed that the BioRID II corresponded to a 35th-45th percentile male in stature, a 35th percentile male in weight; a 96th percentile female in stature and 69th percentile female in weight (Jonsson et al., 2008). The average backsets were 26 mm for females and 63 mm for males in the front seat positions, however smaller differences appeared for the rear passenger position between the BioRID II and the humans (Jonsson et al., 2008). The most significant finding was the difference in backset between a driver with hands on the steering wheel and a front seat passsenger with hands resting in the lap. Differences in backset showed that the standardized seating procedure of the BioRID II more closely resembles the driver position than the front passenger position (Jonsson et al., 2008). The results of this study demonstrated the occupant size coverage of the BioRID II and interesting facts regarding backset for various seating positions in the car, for humans in relation to the BioRID II (Jonsson et al., 2008).

Most of the testing was conducted in the US (vehicle-to-vehicle impacts), Canada, Japan and Europe (sled tests). A decreased gap between the head and the head restraint and the central alignment of the head with the head restraint, has been integral to reducing the risk of whiplash and neck injuries (DeRosia and Yoganandan, 2000). The scientific literature surrounding whiplash and head restraints is extensive. Future work in this area is exciting as technology is constantly improving and several risk factors are being addressed.

Chapter 2

Risk Factors for Whiplash Injury and Associated Disorders

The aim of this section is to provide the reader with the fundamentals and role of epidemiological research in identifying the risk factors for whiplash. Although whiplash injuries are a common outcome of road traffic collisions, there have been very few epidemiological studies that have investigated the risk factors associated with the occurrence of such injuries (Caddy, 1998; Holm et al., 2008; Spitzer et al., 1995). Therefore, existing literature provides limited scientific evidence concerning the factors associated with the risk of whiplash injury (Spitzer et al., 1995). A rear impact collision is a predominant risk factor for whiplash injury. Head restraint positioning and geometry are also key determinants of incurring whiplash injury. The mechanism surrounding a rear-end collision and the resultant whiplash injury is scientifically well established. There are several epidemiological factors and biomechanical theories that can help to explain the mechanism of how a rear-end collision can result in a whiplash injury. The risk factors for whiplash injury from epidemiological studies can be divided into three categories: 1. Individual-related risk factors; 2. Vehicle-related risk factors; 3. Social policy-related risk factors.

1. Individual-Related Risk Factors

a) History of Neck Pain or Injury

Prior research has shown that preconditions of disease are a risk factor for whiplash and WAD (Kivioja, 2004). Specifically, the available research highlights that past history of neck pain (Parmar and Raymakers, 1993; Radanov et al., 1994) and headaches (Kivioja, 2004; Lee, 1999) are risk factors. Additional research also indicates that previous neck pain and headache impact the recovery process (Kivioja, 2004). A study examining the relationships between vehicle and occupant risk factors and the incidence of whiplash in rear-end impact collisions in Adelaide, Australia, identified a history of neck injury as an independent risk factor for whiplash injury (Adjusted odds ratio = 4.50, 95% CI 1.97-10.28) (Caddy 1998; Dolinis, 1997).

The hypothesis underlying this assumption is that any previous injury indicates that the existing tissue has already been weakened by the previous condition (Dolinis, 1997; Jakobsson et al., 2000b). Another possible explanation was that previous injuries weaken the tissues and they do not respond as well as strong tissues (Khan et al., 2000). Some authors have suggested degenerative changes in the cervical spine are associated with an increase in the risk of whiplash (Bogduk and Yoganandan, 2001). Holm, in the most recent best evidence synthesis argues against that association as younger age groups are more likely to seek health care or file a claim for whiplash than older populations, and there is no apparent increased risk of chronicity based on age alone (Holm, 2008).

b) Lower Body Mass Index (BMI)

One study showed that weighing less than 130 pounds was a risk factor for whiplash injury (Banks et al., 2000). The explanation of lower body mass index (BMI) as a risk factor for whiplash injury occurrence is that less weight indicates that the occupant doesn't load the seat back as much or as long, and is thrown forward much more quickly and faster creating higher "G" forces (Banks et al., 2000). An additional study found an increased risk for those with a BMI lower than 25, as they lack fat which could provide a cushion effect and absorb some of the energy of the traffic crash (Zhu et al., 2006).

In addition, related research concerning BMI/head neck index (i.e., decreased risk with increasing mass and neck size) has also been reported in the literature. Fewer neck injuries among people who reported having higher BMI could be due to their small head/torso mass ratio (Boulanger and Rodriguez, 1992; Ryb and Dischinger, 2008; van den Kroonenberg et al., 1998), and the cushion effect, without a significant increase in mass and momentum (Arbabi et al., 2003). Furthermore, research shows that obesity imparts anatomical and physiological changes that may either protect or interfere with the body's response to traffic collision-related injury (Zhu et al., 2006).

c) Tall Drivers/Occupants and Head Restraint Geometry

Head restraints were developed for the 50th percentile of males; therefore drivers/occupants who are significantly taller than the average (e.g., 80th percentile male) are vulnerable to whiplash injuries, since the head restraint geometry is incorrect for their height. The hypothesis underlying this assumption is that tall occupants' head restraints are set too low and this acts as a fulcrum, thereby causing an increased chance of whiplash injury (Lundell et al., 1998; Ono and Kanno, 1996; Viano and Gargan, 1996). Human body characteristics such as height and weight tend to play an important role in traffic collision outcome (Arbabi et al., 2003).

d) Women

Knowledge of individual differences is important when analyzing motor vehicle collision data as well as designing protection systems. Previous literature has consistently found that demographics are a risk factor for whiplash. Several research studies have shown that women are more likely to sustain a neck injury in the event of a rear-end impact (Krafft et al., 2000; Lovsund et al., 1988; Lundell et al., 1998; Minton et al., 1997; Morris and Thomas, 1996; Otte et al., 1997; Spitzer et al., 1995).

The fundamental physiological differences between male and female bodies have been identified as the key reason why women are more vulnerable to whiplash injuries than men. The most prominent findings highlight the vulnerability of women to neck injury as compared to men (Berglund et al., 2003; Chapline et al., 2000; Dolinis, 1997; Huelke and Marsh, 1973; Jakobsson, 2005; Kihlberg, 1969; Krafft et al., 2003; O'Neill et al., 1972).

International research has indicated that females have a somewhat higher relative risk of whiplash injury than males (Berglund et al., 2003; Siegmund et al., 1999). The study by Siegmund and colleagues attempted to control for age, seating position and type of motor vehicle collision. Researchers asserted that anatomical diversities, such as neck strength, smaller muscle mass, and body height account for this sex difference (Berglund et al., 2003; Caddy, 1998; Dolinis, 1997; Siegmund et al., 1999). Australian research also successfully identified female sex as a risk factor for whiplash (Adjusted odds ratio = 2.08, 95% CI 1.13-3.82) (Caddy, 1998; Dolinis, 1997).

These findings are in contrast to population based studies of all-cause motor vehicle collision-related injuries that report a higher incidence of injury among men. The issue of sex and whiplash injury has been debated extensively. This literature demonstrates that women tend to have an increased incidence of both neck pain and whiplash injuries as compared to men (Vasavada et al., 2008). However, there is not a valid model of the female neck that allows for an exploration of sex differences, since researchers have hypothesized that it is not simply a smaller version of the male neck (Vasavada et al., 2008). Earlier work (Langweider et al., 2000) recognized this issue; however the research did not progress until the mid 2000s.

A study that explored this issue demonstrated that sex differences in several neck anthropometry parameters were larger than the differences in head anthropometry parameters (Vasavada et al., 2008). In addition, there were differences in vertebrae size in the anterior-posterior dimension but not in the medial-lateral dimension, and women's necks were found to be significantly weaker than men's. The overall conclusion of the study was that a female-specific model is required to develop and test head restraints since male and female necks are not geometrically similar (Vasavada et al., 2008). In earlier research, Viano and Gargan (1996) also noted that 1 in 5 women sit less than 12 inches away from the steering wheel, which has implications for vehicle seat and head restraint design. Other studies observed that females may be sitting too close to the steering wheel, foot pedal, airbag and/or have improperly fitted shoulder harnesses (Parkin et al., 1995). Knowledge of the demographic differences in vulnerability to whiplash injuries is important when designing effective protection systems. Since females tend to sit higher and closer to the steering wheel, and their back rest angle is more upright, this seating posture results in a slightly higher horizontal shear stress component to the spine in rear-end impacts compared to males (Cullen et al., 1996; McFadden et al., 2000; Parkin et al., 1995). A combination of these factors explains why females are highly vulnerable to whiplash injuries compared to their male counterparts.

In contrast, a systematic review by Scholten-Peeters and colleagues (2003) has counter-claimed the other studies which often mentioned factors like age, sex and compensation as a risk factor for whiplash injuries. This study also claims that these demographic and social policies do not seem to be of any prognostic value (Scholten-Peeters et al., 2003).

However, much of the research on this topic highlights that the differing anatomy is a factor in the higher risk faced by women for whiplash injuries. Studies have found that males have strong neck muscles to counteract the risk of whiplash injury (Vasvada et al., 2008), yet females have longer necks and smaller heads contributing to their higher vulnerability to whiplash injuries in rear-end collisions (Temming and Zobel, 1998). In summary, the majority of the research evidence supports the theory that women are at higher risk for whiplash injury.

2. Vehicle-Related Risk Factors

a) Wearing a Seatbelt

There is a body of literature to suggest that the use of seatbelts prevents all other severe injuries, yet it actually increases the likelihood of injuries to the cervical spine. Several studies have concluded that wearing a seatbelt is a risk factor for whiplash injury (Allen et al., 1985; Borchgrevink et al., 1996; Deans et al., 1987; Dunn and Blazer, 1987; Evans, 1996; Hayes et al., 1991; Kallieris et al., 1991; Lange and Voas, 1998; Morris and Thomas, 1996; Mulhall et al., 2003; NASS, 1991; Nygren, 1984; Ommaya et al., 1982; Richter et al., 2000; Roh and Fazzalaro, 1993; Satoh et al., 1997; Teifke et al., 1993; Versteegen et al., 1998).

Conversely, there is also research that indicates that wearing a seatbelt is not a risk factor for whiplash injury. A recent case control study that utilized data from France and Spain contradicts many previous risk-related epidemiological studies by showing that wearing a seatbelt, being in a heavier car, and being older than 65 years of age were protective factors for whiplash injury and were associated with a lower risk of whiplash injury (Martin et al., 2008).

Regardless of the uncertainty of seatbelt use and whiplash injury, all occupants of motor vehicles should heed the ubiquitous message that proper seatbelt use is a highly effective means of reducing the risk of injury in general, and specifically reduces the risk of fatal injury.

b) Drivers and Front-Seated Occupants

Whiplash injury appears to be predominantly an injury issue for drivers and front seated occupants, as literature on the risk for rear-seated passengers is sparse. Consistent with other findings, Berglund and colleagues (2003) found that drivers had a higher risk of incurring a whiplash injury compared to rear-seated passengers (1.78; 95% CI 1.60-1.97) (Berglund et al., 2003). Similarly, additional studies have confirmed these findings indicating that the risk of whiplash injury is lowest for the rear-seated passengers and highest for drivers and front-seated occupants (Carlsson et al., 1995; Jakobsson et al., 2000b; Krafft et al., 2003; Lövsund et al., 1988; Otremski et al., 1989; Pamar and Raymakers, 1993; States et al., 1972). An explanation for the increased risk could be due to a more rigid, uniform and less elastic design of the rear seats than the front seats (Pamar and Raymakers, 1993). Additional proposed hypotheses for the increased risk of whiplash for drivers and front-seated occupants include the differences in seat back resistance and the potential to strike something (Carlsson et al., 1995; Kihlberg, 1969; Lövsund et al., 1988; Otremski, 1989; Otte et al., 1985; Pamar and Raymakers, 1993; States et al., 1972).

Volvo collision statistics reported a significantly higher risk of the driver sustaining a neck injury than the passengers (Lundell et al., 1998). Researchers hypothesized that the differences between the driver and front seated passenger could be due to different seating postures (Lundell et al., 1998). Drivers are more prone to bend forward and away from the seat backrest and head restraint than passengers, who are more relaxed and probably more likely to rest their head against the head restraint.

However, in contradiction, Krafft and colleagues (2003) found that when crash pulse and occupant seating positioning were controlled for, whiplash injury risk was higher for rear passengers in rear-end collisions (Krafft et al., 2003).

c) Mass of the Striking Vehicle

There is literature that demonstrates that impact by a striking vehicle of greater mass (i.e., 25% greater mass) (Force = Mass x Acceleration) is a risk factor for whiplash injuries (Caddy, 1998; Chapline et al., 2000; Dolinis, 1997; Kornhauser, 1996; Wood, 1997). Studies that examined side impact crashes also confirmed that the mass of the striking vehicle is a risk factor for severe injuries and fatalities (Desapriya et al., 2006; Evans and Frick, 1992; 1993).

d) Speed of the Striking Vehicle

In a series of human volunteer collision tests of low speed rear impact collisions, it was reported that the threshold for cervical spine soft tissue injury was 5 mph, and most injuries occur at speeds below 12 mph (Morris and Thomas, 1996; Olsson et al., 1990; Siegmund et al., 1999). Interestingly, epidemiological studies have shown that most rear impact collisions causing injury occur at crash speeds of 6 to 12 mph, which is below the threshold for property damage to the vehicle (Scholten-Peeters et al., 2003).

Often in other traffic collision-related injuries, speed is highlighted as a risk factor for collision outcome, and the risk of injury severity and fatality are increased in high velocity compared to low velocity collisions. In contrast, a collision speed under 10 mph (low speed crashes) increased the risk of whiplash injuries. In slow speed collisions, the car does not crush or crumple therefore the energy is transferred to the occupant and is not absorbed by the car (Foret-Bruno et al., 1991).

Muscular strain may also occur as the muscles tighten during the early part of the collision as the head extends backward (Gross et al., 1996; Hurwitz et al., 1996). During low speed collisions rapid pressure changes in the spinal canal can create a great deal of strain on the spinal nerve roots which in turn can result in pain symptoms after a low speed collision (Aker et al., 1996).

e) Impact Direction of the Vehicle

According to a best evidence synthesis by Holm and colleagues (2008), few factors related to the collision itself (for example, direction of the collision, head rest type) were predictive of whiplash injury.

Whiplash injuries occur most commonly due to rear impact collisions. However, a contradictory finding surfaced showing that the absolute number of whiplash cases was greater in front and side impact collisions than rear-end collisions in France and Spain (Martin et al., 2008). Additional evidence was found to support this finding indicating that whiplash injuries occurred not only in rear-end collisions but also in other types of traffic collisions (Björnstig et al., 1990; Bogduk and Yoganandan, 2001; Cassidy et al., 2000; Deans et al., 1986; Hildingsson and Toolanen, 1990; Jakobsson et al., 2000b). However, confirming most international studies, research in Sweden showed that rear-end collisions were associated with the highest relative risk of whiplash injury when compared with side impacts (1.82; 95% CI 1.68-1.96) (Berglund et al., 2003).

f) Extent of Vehicle Deformation

There is a common belief that occupant injury correlates to the amount of damage to the vehicle in all types of collisions. However, the literature on this issue is quite clear and states that there is absolutely no correlation between the amount of damage to the car and the risk of injury (Hurwitz et al., 1996). Contrary to existing literature, one study found that vehicle damage severity is a risk factor for whiplash injuries and a crucial factor in whiplash injury recovery (Hijioka et al., 2001).

However, most of the literature determined that a vehicle with less damage may result in higher forces experienced by the driver and occupants compared with a vehicle with extensive damage (Berglund et al., 2003). According to research evidence, severity measures based on deformation depth has not been identified as a good predictor of whiplash injury risk (Jakobsson, 2000b). This is related to the literature on speed that indicates that the risk of whiplash injury is higher in low velocity collisions at speeds of 6 to 12 mph (Scholten-Peeters et al., 2003).

g) Stiff Vehicle Structure

There are some epidemiological studies to support the assumption that stiffer vehicles are a risk factor for whiplash. The injury mechanism occurs because the stiffer vehicle bounces in response to a collision rather than absorbing the energy of the impact (Gross et al., 1996; Hurwitz et al., 1996; Olsson et al., 1990). Vehicles with stiff rear-end structures and/or seatbacks produce greater torso accelerations, making it harder to keep the driver's head and torso moving together. It is the rapid acceleration of the head in relation to the torso that results in whiplash (Gross et al., 1996; Hurwitz et al., 1996).

Compatibility is important in order to secure mutual protection in collisions between large and small vehicles. To enhance compatibility, good structural interaction and stiffness matching are important elements (Hasegawa and Kudoh, 2009). In recent years, light truck vehicles (LTVs) have been infiltrating the traditional vehicle fleet that had previously been dominated by smaller cars. This new trend has created vehicle compatibility issues in motor vehicle collisions. When smaller cars are hit by LTVs, these crashes result in a disproportionate number of injuries and fatalities to the occupants of the smaller vehicles (Desapriya et al., 2006). In order to reduce the effects of incompatibility, car manufacturers have increased the structural stiffness of vehicles as a crash mitigating factor (Linder and Avery, 2004). Comparisons of vehicle accelerations and additional parameters have identified an increase in vehicle structural stiffness in vehicles manufactured between 1980 and 2001 (Linder and Avery, 2004). Vehicle stiffness is a risk factor for whiplash and related injuries, and therefore becomes problematic in attempts to mitigate these types of injuries (Linder and Avery, 2004; Richter et al., 2004; Sendur et al., 2005).

Researchers reported that vehicle structures have been getting stiffer since the mid 1990s and this trend is continuing (Richter et al., 2004; Sendur et al., 2005). Stiff vehicles that do not absorb sufficient collision forces in low-speed impacts may reduce vehicular damages, but they transmit increased crash forces to occupants, increasing the risk of injuries, particularly whiplash. A study was conducted that was limited to an impact magnitude of 10 kph as total energy was held constant, indicating that Delta-V was 10 kph. Results showed that vehicle stiffness had a strong influence on the retraction (70%), rebound (43%), and protraction (47%) phases of motion (Sendur et al., 2005). Headrestraint backset demonstrated a strong influence on the extension (49%) and rebound (39%) phases. This study emphasized that a vehicle should be viewed as a system in which there are complex interactions among the vehicle, seat, and occupant, which are all risk factors for whiplash injuries (Sendur et al., 2005). This calls into question past policies that limited compensation primarily based on the extent of vehicular damage sometimes referred to as, "no crash no cash" rather than consider the crash and safety characteristics of specific vehicles (make, model and year).

h) Poor Quality Seats

Farmer and colleagues (2008) noted that the seats rated as "poor" by the Insurance Institute for Highway Safety's (IIHS) seat evaluation tended to increase the risk of whiplash injuries and longer term disability (Farmer et al., 2008). The stiffness of the seat and head restraint is also highlighted as a risk factor (Viano, 2003a, 2003b). However, a study by Szabo and colleagues (2003) contended that seat and head restraints were not factors in increasing the risk for whiplash injuries (Szabo et al., 2003). Although the majority of the research contends that the quality of the seat is an important risk factor for mitigating the occurrence of whiplash injury, studies do appear with contradictory findings.

3. Social Policy-Related Risk Factors

a) The Existing Insurance Compensation System

There is sparse literature in the area of insurance compensation systems and the effect on whiplash injury. A review by Spitzer and colleagues (1995) reported varying annual incidence rates for whiplash injury ranging from 70 to 700 per

100,000 population in Canadian provinces. They indicated that these provincial (as well as international) prevalence rates are likely influenced by the legal/administrative provisions in operation in each jurisdiction (Spitzer et al., 1995). The study revealed that in jurisdictions with a 'no-fault' insurance provision (particularly those jurisdictions that could limit tort actions), there were lower claim rates for whiplash injuries (Spitzer et al., 1995).

A study conducted in the Canadian province of Saskatchewan demonstrated a 28% reduction in the incidence of WAD after insurance payments for pain and suffering were eliminated (Cassidy et al., 2000). This included claims, as well as all those requiring treatment for their neck injury. In addition, there was a 54% decrease in the time-to-claim closure after this policy change (Cassidy et al., 2000). Importantly, removal of compensation payments for pain and suffering for whiplash injury resulted in a substantial decline in the number of persons seeking care and a substantial improvement in recovery times (Cassidy et al., 2000). It is important that public health policies promote prevention and recovery from conditions such as whiplash or WAD and not create incentives for illness-promoting behavior, or inappropriate and excessive individual care (Cassidy et al., 2000; Holm et al., 2008).

There is a lack of extensive population-level research on whiplash and WAD and insurance policy changes; however, the available limited research shows a positive relationship among whiplash compensation availability and injury prevalence.

Gaps in the Literature

A best evidence synthesis by Holm and colleagues (2008) highlighted the important gaps in the literature including risk factors for whiplash injuries and also showed that evidence regarding risk factors is inadequate and insufficient (Holm et al., 2008). Accordingly, investigators urged that more research using population-based whiplash risk data should be conducted and designed to strictly control for possible confounding factors using accurate denominators (Holm et al., 2008).

An additional best evidence synthesis by Guzman and colleagues (2008) also reported gaps in the literature concerning the frequency of risk factors, assessment, intervention course and prognostic factors for neck pain and its associated disorders, including whiplash injuries and that only 46% of the scientific literature on neck pain/whiplash was judged to be scientifically valid (Guzman et al., 2008).

A thorough examination of research databases, various papers, and the grey literature, revealed that compared to developed countries, there has been no epidemiological research available concerning whiplash and related risk factors common to populations living in developing countries. Most of the available literature focused on the epidemiological issues related to North American and European populations. There were a limited number of studies available that explored populations in Japan, Australia and New Zealand. The global burden of disease studies have repeatedly projected that traffic-related injuries will become the third largest contributor to global death and disability by the year 2020 (Murray, 2006; Murray and Lopez, 1996). The studies logically argue that much of the burden of traffic collisions in the future will remain in developing countries due to rapid motorization, lack of infrastructure development, and lack of prevention and treatment strategies. Therefore, future whiplash injury prevention efforts should be extended to explore the current status and epidemiology of these types of injuries in developing countries.

The development of strategies for future whiplash injury prevention in developing countries, as well as all of the above challenges should be addressed. Simultaneously, it is important for the field of whiplash injury epidemiology to move away from the largely descriptive studies with considerably small sample sizes that have been predominant in the literature, to the application of more rigorous analytical methods to identify demographic, vehicle and environmental risk factors for whiplash injuries. New advances in the prevention of whiplash injuries will continue to require a more analytical approach in order to understand the complex array of factors that influence the mechanism, severity, and outcomes of injury.

Chapter 3

KNOWLEDGE AND AWARENESS OF CORRECT HEAD RESTRAINT POSITIONING

KNOWLEDGE AND AWARENESS STUDIES

Many drivers do not correctly adjust their head restraints due to a lack of awareness of the consequences of incorrect adjustment. Surveys conducted on the general population demonstrated that they were unaware of the protective value of head restraints and believed that their current head restraint adjustment was adequate (Brown and Nepomuceno, 1999). Observational research in Canada, the UK, the US and Europe show that there is low awareness about the protective value of head restraints and that most drivers and occupants in vehicles with adjustable head restraints have not adjusted them appropriately according to scientific guidelines (Braddick and Love, 1990; Chaplin et al., 2000; Cullen et al., 1996; Garret and Morris 1972; Hong, 2004; Johnson, 1996; Lubin and Sehmer 1993; Mahaffey et al., 2002; Nygren et al., 1985; O'Neill et al., 1972; Parkin et al., 1995; Pedder and Hillebrandt, 2000; Saab et al., 2000; Taylor et al., 2005; Viano and Gargan, 1996; Young et al., 2005). Current research suggests that serious neck injuries and associated disability can be reduced by 35% if the gap between what is known by high quality research and what is actually carried out in policy and practice can be reduced (Farmer et al., 2008; Zuby and Lund, 2007).

Research from the early 1970s to late 1990s investigated people's awareness and practices concerning head restraint adjustment while driving. O'Neill and colleagues (1972) demonstrated that 78% of drivers had incorrectly positioned their head restraint, while Garrett and Morris (1972) found that 73% of adjustable head restraints were left in the down position. This was consistent into the mid

1980s as Nygren and colleagues (1985) showed that 83% of adjustable head restraints were in the down position during driving. In the early 1990s the percentage of drivers with head restraints in the down position, decreased to 62% (Lubin and Sehmer, 1993). The percentage increased once again into the mid 1990s as Viano and Gargan reported that 83% of adjustable head restraints could have been raised for better protection of the driver (Viano and Gargan, 1996).

A survey revealed that less than half of drivers in British Columbia, Canada believed that incorrectly adjusted head restraints have an impact on insurance and health care costs (Fockler et al., 1998). Furthermore, over one-third of the respondents were not confident in their knowledge of the consequences of incorrectly adjusted head restraints. In the same survey, drivers were also asked to provide reasons for adjusting their head restraints. The most frequently reported reasons involved comfort, not safety. These results further underscore the need for increased recognition by the driving public, of the consequences of incorrectly adjusted head restraints (Fockler et al., 1998).

A number of studies have reported that adjustable head restraints are often improperly positioned by drivers (Cullen et al., 1996; Nygren et al., 1985; Viano and Gargan, 1995). Therefore, a comparison of adjustable head restraint designs must take into account the positioning of the head restraint relative to the driver's head both in the adjusted and unadjusted situations. In one study, greater than 70% (117) of the vehicles received poor evaluations of head restraint positioning (Viano and Gargan, 1995). Braddick and Love (1990) found that only 33% of head restraints were correctly adjusted in the UK (Braddick and Love, 1990).

In the fall of 1995, the National Highway Traffic Safety Administration (NHTSA) conducted a survey of the positions of the occupant's head relative to the head restraint in 282 vehicles. Of these vehicles, 23% had fixed head restraints, with 77% of these restraints positioned at or above the occupants' ears. A lower percentage (59%) of the 77% of adjustable head restraints was positioned at or above the occupants' ears. About half of the adjustable head restraints were left in the lowest position (NHTSA, 1996).

O'Neill et al. (1972) observed drivers in 4,983 moving domestic passenger cars in the metropolitan areas of Los Angeles, CA, and Washington, DC. In Los Angeles, 57% of the women and 74% of the men had adjustable head restraints that were positioned incorrectly. Results indicated that more than half of the adjustable head restraints were incorrectly positioned (O'Neill et al., 1972).

Observation of 992 motor vehicles revealed that most drivers do not have their head restraints effectively positioned (Lubin and Sehmer, 1993). Improper positioning was more common with adjustable restraints, in commercial vehicles, and among male drivers. They found that only 40.3% of adjustable head restraints were positioned properly. This research also demonstrated that 30.2% of male drivers had correctly positioned the head restraints compared to 67.6% of females (Lubin and Sehmer, 1993).

A survey of drivers by Parkin and colleagues (1995) (involving 1,000 drivers and 19 different car models) in the UK found that 50% of the driving population had the head restraint positioned greater than 15 cm (6 in.) from the backs of their heads, horizontally. Drivers were filmed using a video camera equipped with a high speed shutter as they passed a white screen. Three separate locations were used, in which the camera could not be viewed by the drivers. This study found that only 5% of drivers had their head restraint correctly positioned vertically, with the great majority having it positioned too low. Fifty percent of the population had the head restraint positioned 10 cm (4 in.) or more below the center of the head. Currently, only a small proportion of drivers (7%) meet these standards in Portland, Oregon. Fixed head restraints were three times more likely to be optimally positioned than adjustable head restraints (Young et al., 2005).

The Insurance Corporation of British Columbia (ICBC) conducted a survey in 1996, in the Lower Mainland of British Columbia, Canada to evaluate the positioning of head restraints. The results showed that 57% of drivers with adjustable head restraints had them positioned incorrectly (Geddes et al., 1997).

The Insurance Bureau of Canada (IBC) conducted a study that rated the head restraint position of 7,571 drivers and 1,090 passengers from seven Canadian provinces as 'good', 'marginal', 'poor' or 'very poor'. Results showed that only 14% of drivers and 19% of front seat passengers had their head restraint in a position rated as 'good', and that for 53% of the drivers, the adjustment was so inadequate that it would have offered no protection in a rear-end collision (Mahaffey et al., 2002). Evidence shows that the typical driver and many professionals have poor knowledge of the correct use of head restraints. A cross-sectional study showed that even chiropractic interns' knowledge and application of correct head restraint positioning is lacking (Taylor et al., 2005). The study by IBC noted that drivers of large cars and light trucks were significantly below the average for properly adjusted head restraints (6% and 4% respectively compared to the 14% average) illustrating a large variation due to vehicle type (Mahaffey et al., 2002). This poses a safety concern as these vehicle types typically constitute a major component of the fleet driven by those in businesses, utilities and public service agencies (such as police, fire, government).

Table 2 provides a summary of the international observational and knowledge and awareness studies regarding the incorrect use of head restaints.

Table 2. International observational and knowledge and awareness studies – Incorrect use of head restraints

Study	Methods	Participants	Results	Quality of the study
O'Neill et al., 1972 (USA)	Observational survey (convenience sample)	3345 males and 1638 female drivers	84% of male drivers and 71% of female drivers incorrectly positioned their head restraints	Moderate
Garret and Morris, 1972 (USA)	Observational survey (convenience sample)	237 vehicles	73% of drivers incorrectly positioned their head restraints	Moderate
Nygren et al., 1985 (Sweden)	Traffic crash data analysis	187 vehicles	83% of drivers incorrectly positioned their head restraints	Moderate
Braddick and Love, 1990 (UK)	Observational survey/ questionnaire (convenience sample)	150 male drivers	136 drivers knew that head restraints were a safety feature; only 24% identified correct position of the head restraint; 33% correctly adjusted the head restraint	Moderate
Lubin and Sehmer, 1993 (Canada)	Parking lot survey/ Roadside observational survey	708 vehicles in a parking lot/ 879 vehicles in motion (61.9% males and 38.1% women)	In a parking lot survey- 62% of the adjustable headrests were in the down position; in a roadside observational survey 46.3% of drivers' head restraints were adjusted correctly. Female drivers are more than twice as likely as males to have their head restraints positioned correctly.	Moderate
Parkin et al., 1995 (UK)	Roadside observational study	1000 drivers (75.8% male and 24.2% females) Random sample of vehicles	50% of the driver population had correctly adjusted their head restraints horizontally. Only 5% had correctly adjusted them vertically	Moderate
Cullen et al., 1996 (USA and UK)	Cross national study	Information on sample size not available	88% of UK passengers, 97% of US drivers and 91% of US passengers had their restraint positioned inappropriately	Moderate

NHTSA, 1996 (USA)	Parking lot survey	Convenience sample of drivers (282)	47% of adjustable restraints were left in their lowest position. 26% of these were sufficiently high to have the top of the restraint above or at the top of the ear. 51% were not in their lowest position. 30% were below the top of the ear. 2% of all adjustable restraint cases could not be assessed. Drivers had not perceived the head restraint as a protective device, but simply as a head rest or pillow.	Good
Viano and Gargan, 1996 (USA)	Observational survey (convenience sample)	Convenience sample of vehicles (1915)	10% of drivers had adjusted their head restraints correctly. 14.8% of women and 6.1% of men had a favourable, yet not absolutely correct head rest position.	Good
Johnson, 1996 (Canada)	Awareness survey (convenience sample)	338 Canadian medical students, 183 family doctors, and 45 trauma team members were asked about health promotion items. None included the topic of head rest adjustment as a health promotion item to improve traffic safety in youth.	Only 18% of family practice instructors in a University of Toronto network agreed that they would counsel youth about proper adjustment of head restraints. Shocking results were found in this survey and the trauma team members did not expect primary care physicians to include head restraint position as an important item in health promotion.	Good
Saab et al., 2000 (Lebanon)	Observational survey (convenience sample)	Convenience sample of drivers (2105)	32.2% had their head restraints adequately adjusted.	Moderate
Pedder and Hillebrandt, 2000 (Canada)	Crash vehicle and driver interviews and vehicle head restraint position inspection	Selected claim centers of 3 provincial insurance agencies in Canada: ICBC; Manitoba Public Insurance; Saskatchewan Government Insurance. Random sample of 1,094 rear-ended vehicles. Position of driver's head relative to the head restraint was measured.	20.8% had their head restraints correctly adjusted horizontally (a "good" rating using ICBC protocols). 37.8% had their head restraints correctly adjusted vertically (combining ICBC "good," "acceptable" and "marginal" vertical separations).	

Table 2. (Continued)

		Head restraint position was also measured using the ICBC Head Restraint Measuring Device (HRMD)		Good
Chapline et al., 2000 (USA)	Crash vehicle and driver interviews and vehicle head restraint position inspection	585 read-end collisions	Only 11% had adequately positioned head restraints and women with adequately adjusted head restraints were less likely to report neck pain (29%) than women with poorly adjusted head restraints (52%).	Moderate
Mahaffey et al., 2002 (Canada)	Observational survey (convenience sample)	7571 drivers and 1090 passengers	46 % had their head restraints adequately adjusted. Females had correctly adjusted their head restraint at twice the rate of males. 60% of passengers had their head restraints adequately adjusted.	Good
Hong, 2004 (Korea)	Interview and observational survey	1100 vehicles/ drivers	19% had their head restraints adequately adjusted.	Moderate
Young et al., 2005 (USA)	Observational and awareness survey	4287 drivers/ 51 survey respondents	7% had their head restraints adequately adjusted. The questionnaire results indicated that: the head restraint is a safety device to prevent neck injuries (75%). However 55% of respondents had never adjusted the head restraints.	Good
Taylor et al., 2005 (Canada)	Awareness survey	30 chiropractic interns	Only 13.3% of chiropractic interns knew the recommended vertical distance and only 20% knew the recommended horizontal distance for head restraints.	Good

Based on the review of the literature presented in this section, there is a significant lack of public awareness surrounding the proper use and correct adjustment of head restraints. It is not only the general public who are unaware of correct positioning, but also those in the medical profession (Johnson, 1996; Taylor et al., 2005). This may be due to lack of, or ineffective education, engineering, enforcement, media, and social marketing preventative efforts.

Chapter 4

EVOLUTION OF CHANGES IN REGULATIONS, STANDARDS, AND POLICY FOR HEAD RESTRAINTS

This section focuses primarily on the US, Canada, and Europe, and describes how the standards from different countries were harmonized to develop a global technical regulation on head restraints. A summary of the various vehicle rating systems for head restraints is also provided. Table 3 provides a brief summary of the standards, regulations, ratings, and milestones surrounding head restraints.

Table 3. Summary of Standards, Regulations, Ratings, and Milestones

Standard/Regulation	Year implemented
US Federal Motor Vehicle Safety Standard 202 (US FMVSS 202) (Minimum height of 700 mm)	1969
Canadian Standards (Same as above)	1978
European Standards (Minimum height of 750 mm, adjustable to 800 mm)	1978
IIWPG formed IIWPG/RCAR ratings created	2000
NHTSA issued notice of proposed rulemaking -US FMVSS 202a	2001-2004
Folksam Insurance and Swedish Road Authority (SRA) published seat/head restraint rating systems	2003
Ad Hoc Group on Head Restraints created (directed by UNECE)	2004
EuroNCAP ratings – amalgamation of RCAR/IIWPG and Swedish rating (SRA) systems	2008
All new US vehicles required to meet updated guidelines (FMVSS 202a) (Minimum height of 750 mm, adjustable to 800 mm, minimum backset of 55 mm)	2009 (September)
International Global Technical Regulation for Head Restraints	Pending

Standards and Regulations

Vehicle manufacturers have been required to equip vehicles with head restraints since 1969 in the US, and since 1978 in Canada and in Europe. The European regulations include a minimum height of 750 mm (29.5 in) and restraints must be adjustable to 800 mm (31.5 in) above the seating reference point.

The US Motor Vehicle Safety Standard 202, in effect from 1969 to September 2009, required that head restraints be adjustable to a height of 700 mm (27.6 in) above the position of the center of rotation of the hip joint when a person is seated in the vehicle (seating reference point) (Kahane, 1982). This was problematic because the head restraints were not as high as the center of gravity of an average male's head.

In Canada, the safety standard enacted in 1978 was aligned with the US requirements for head restraints. The final rule modifying the requirements of safety standard 202 of the US was published in December 2004, and amended in May 2007. The new requirements increased the minimum height of the outboard head restraints from 700 to 750 mm, and introduced a maximum backset requirement, maximum gap requirement between the head restraint and seat and required testing for height retention and energy absorption (Department of Transport, 2008). There were also more stringent testing requirements for strength testing and backset retention and a new dynamic testing protocol with updated male test dummies (Department of Transport, 2008).

The amendment that is proposed for 2009 in both the US and in Canada, is a stepping stone toward international harmonization of head restraint requirements (Department of Transport, 2008), that will be developed as a global technical regulation.

An ad hoc informal working group on head restraints has been meeting since 2004 to discuss and evaluate issues surrounding the requirement of head restraints in vehicles, with the main goal of making recommendations concerning the development of a global technical regulation for head restraints. At a meeting in June 2006, the group began developing a proposal for a draft global technical regulation that was based on the requirements of the United Nations Economic Commission for Europe's (UNECE) Regulation 17, Regulation 25, and the upgraded FMVSS 202 (FMVSS 202a).

The group made several recommendations for the development of a global technical regulation, which are summarized below (Ad hoc Group on Head Restraints, Meeting Minutes June 23, 2006).

Head Restraint Height:

For front outboard head restraint height, the recommendation was to increase to 850 mm above the reference point to accomodate taller populations. However, based on the evidence, it was determined that the current 800 mm was sufficient to protect the 95th percentile Netherlands male (tallest in the world). For rear outboard head restraint height, a 750 mm minimum height and static requirements, excluding backset was recommended. For front center, it was recommended that the head restraint conform to the same regulations as the rear outboard head restraints (optional, no backset requirement, 750 mm height). For the rear center, the requirements were the same as front center, although no height requirement was necessary (Ad hoc Group on Head Restraints, Meeting Minutes June 23, 2006).

Backset:

In 2004, discussions continued on this parameter. There was concensus that a recommendation for backset was important, yet the 55 mm requirement may be too stringent. Issues arose regarding measurement methods and occupant comfort levels (Ad hoc Group on Head Restraints, Meeting Minutes June 23, 2006).

Dynamic Test:

An optional dynamic test was proposed as an option to the static requirements. Concerns arose surrounding which type of dummy to use. The Hybrid III dummy spine is not humanlike, nor is its motion during a dynamic test; however, the BioRID dummy, although preferred, is not ready to be made part of a regulation. It was decided that the dynamic test could be phased into the proposal at a later time (Ad hoc Group on Head Restraints, Meeting Minutes June 23, 2006).

At the group's seventh meeting, Canadian representatives presented their findings on the use of the Head Restraint Measuring Device (HRMD), created by the Insurance Corporation of British Columbia (ICBC), which was used for measuring backset. The testing confirmed that the HRMD provides repeatable and reproducible results, and that increasing the number of measurements reduces the backset variability (Gane and Pedder, 1996). The global technical regulation will include the use of the HRMD (Department of Transport, 2008).

The work of this group has now led to agreement regarding the parameters of a global technical regulation for head restraints, which was approved in March 2008. Due to non-consensus regarding dynamic testing only quasi-static testing requirements will be included in the global technical regulation. Work is underway to develop an internationally accepted dynamic testing protocol (Department of Transport, 2008).

In the US, 2009 will be a pivotal year for head restraints and and the prevention of whiplash. All 2009 vehicle models must include the mandated requirements of head restraints to all front seats as well as back seats. These include: a minimum of 29.5 inches (750 mm) from an occupant's hip to the top of the head restraint and the backset must be 2 inches (50.8 mm) between the head and the head restraint (IIHS, 2005).

BENEFITS OF HARMONIZATION

The approved harmonization of standards and regulations into a global technical regulation combined elements from the UNECE Regulations No.17, No. 25, and the newly upgraded US FMVSS 202a. International motor vehicle manufacturers, along with the entire industry benefit from harmonization and new technology-based improvements to the head restraint regulations. The benefits to industry include the improved safety of the head restraints, leveraging of resources, and the harmonization of requirements. Industry also benefits from a reduction in the cost of development, testing and the fabrication process of new vehicle models. Consumers worldwide benefit by having a choice of vehicles built to higher, globally recognized standards, providing an improved level of safety at a lower cost.

SAFETY RATINGS

The regulations for head restraints were not completely effective in rear collisions, which lead to enormous costs for insurance companies; therefore, whiplash received considerable attention. It was a significant issue for insurance companies, vehicle manufacturers had to design improved head restraints that were appropriate for the majority of the driving and occupant population, and there was consumer pressure. This requirement has resulted in numerous rating systems for seats and head restraints (Avery et al., 2007). The current ratings include: the International Insurance Whiplash Prevention Group (IIWPG) ratings, the Swedish Road Administration (SRA) ratings, Federal Motor Vehicle Safety Standard (FMVSS) ratings and more recently, the European New Car Assessment Programme (Euro NCAP) ratings, which are a combination of the IIWPG and SRA systems.

IIWPG Rating System

The IIWPG utilizes a two-stage process for evaluating and rating the ability of seats and head restraints to prevent neck injury in moderate and low-speed rear-end impacts (IIWPG, 2004). First, the static geometry of the head restraint is measured and rated; second, a dynamic evaluation in a simulated rear-end collision is conducted and rated. The static geometry measurements include height and horizontal distance to the back of the head. Head restraints with geometric ratings of 'acceptable' or 'good', then go on to dynamic testing in a simulated 16 km/h rear impact to obtain a rating for how well the torso, neck and head are supported (IIWPG, 2004). The results of the geometric measurements and the dynamic testing are combined to produce an overall rating of the seat and head restraint as a whole (IIWPG, 2004). The dynamic testing involves seat design parameters (time-to-head restraint contact; energy-absorbing characteristics) and test dummy response parameters (neck shear force; neck tension force).

Initial Geometry	Dynamic Test Results					FINAL RATING
	HR Contact Time T_{HRC}	Torso Acceleration T1g	Neck Shear Fx	Neck Tension Fz	Summary Dynamic Performance	
Good	≤ 70 ms	any value	≤ 130 N	≤ 600 N	Pass	GOOD
	any value	≤ 9 g				
	> 70 ms	> 9 g	any value	any value	3.1.1.1 Fail	ACCEPTABLE
Height ≥ -6 cm Backset ≤ 7 cm	any value	any value	> 130 N	any value		
	any value	any value	any value	> 600 N		
Acceptable	≤ 70 ms	Any T1g	≤ 130 N	≤ 600 N	Pass	
	Any T_{HRC}	≤ 9 g				
	> 70 ms	> 9 g	any value	any value	Fail	MARGINAL
Height ≥ -8 cm Backset ≤ 9 cm	any value	any value	> 130 N	any value		
	any value	any value	Any value	> 600 N		
Marginal Height ≥ -10 cm Backset ≤ 11 cm	No Dynamic Test					
Poor Height ≤ -10 cm Backset > 11 cm						POOR

(Source: European Enhanced Vehicle-safety Committee (EEVC), WG 20, March 2005, pp. 21).

Figure 1. IIWPG Rating Matrix.

Chapter 5

STRATEGIES TO REDUCE WHIPLASH INJURIES AND FUTURE DIRECTIONS

IMPROVEMENTS IN SYSTEMATIC REVIEW METHODS

An international team of experts who completed a Cochrane systematic review in 2007 found insufficient scientifically rigorous evidence to accurately assess the effectiveness of most existing therapies for whiplash injuries due to methodological issues precluding the pooling of data given clinical and statistical heterogeneity (Verhagen et al., 2007a; 2007b). The authors found that individual studies demonstrated effectiveness of one treatment over another, but the comparisons were varied and the results inconsistent. Therefore, using a Cochrane systematic synthesis framework, the authors concluded the evidence neither supports nor refutes the effectiveness of either passive or active treatments to relieve the symptoms of WAD, Grades 1 or 2.

The most recent systematic review used a best-evidence synthesis approach and made recommendations of therapeutic treatments that are "likely helpful", "possibly helpful", "likely not helpful" or "not enough evidence to make determination". These two systematic appraisal methods have fundamentally different approaches to assessing the methodologic quality and can contribute to differences in their conclusions. Differences in systematic appraisal methods are particularly important when research data cannot be pooled and when there is a lack of sufficient high quality studies to inform best practices.

Van der Velde and colleagues (2007) found that both the Cochrane and Best-Evidence Synthesis approaches rely on the level of expertise and composition of reviewers. They found that Cochrane suffers from an overreliance of checklists that can inadvertently create an artificial bias in appraising the quality of studies.

For instance, Cochrane reviewers use an 11-item checklist to assess quality of studies including (i) blinding of caregivers and (ii) blinding of subjects. In a study assessing the value of exercise under the Cochrane review process this would lead to a two point deduction without considering issues related to internal validity and study purpose. In a similar way, Cochrane checklists can inadvertently inflate the quality rating if the study reports on outcome measures without considering the validity of the outcome measures used. Olsen and colleagues assessed a sample of Cochrane reviews and highlighted other areas where improvements are needed. They found that 29% of reviews had major problems, including inappropriate methods and conclusions (Olsen et al., 2001). We would support Olsen and colleagues' suggestion that users of any systematic review should assess its reliability thoroughly before adoption of recommendations in to policy-making decisions.

Best evidence synthesis approaches suffer from a less structured approach and require readers to accept that reviewers have a higher level of scientific and clinical judgment to weigh the strengths and weaknesses of studies across a broad range of parameters to consider the scientific merit of the research design, methods used, data collected, analysis and conclusions. Best-evidence synthesis methods require a much larger investment both financially and in terms of human resources. The Bone and Joint Decade Task Force on Neck Pain took seven years to complete the best evidence synthesis and associated studies as well as required extensive group participation of reviewers and advisory committees through its deliberations.

Fundamentally there is a stronger need for greater coordination and collaboration within the whiplash research community to create a more systematic roadmap to answer important questions regarding whiplash treatment.

We know that the basic requirement to reduce the risk of whiplash injury was identified in the 1960s. However, the proper positioning of head restraints has not being achieved to date (O'Neill, 2000). O'Neill (2000) raised a very interesting question: Why has there been a failure in the dissemination of the accumulated wealth of knowledge, even 40 years later? As a result, whiplash has been cited as the single most common non-fatal injury diagnosis reported by Emergency Department physicians in the US (Halping et al., 2009). Recent research also shows that although whiplash injuries are common, there are few robust randomized trials to inform practice (Lamb et al., 2009).

There are several gaps and areas with inconclusive evidence in the literature that require attention. There is also a lack of knowledge and understanding of neck injury mechanisms, creating a major obstacle in producing an effective countermeasure. If evidence shows that currently available treatment strategies are not effective in reducing whiplash related pain, suffering and long term disability, it is obvious that increased efforts for the prevention of whiplash injuries are required.

FUTURE RESEARCH – FILLING THE GAPS

Women

First and foremost, there is no conclusive evidence concerning why women are highly vulnerable to whiplash injuries. We appeal to the international research community to conduct additional research to widen the scope of this issue that could help identify demographic risk factors of whiplash injuries or to investigate why women are more vulnerable to whiplash injuries in rear end collisions. Most of the currently available treatment strategies for whiplash injuries are not always effective. Doctors commonly prescribe cervical collars fo keep the neck stable, yet the collars have little effect on the range of motion of the neck, and by promoting inactivity, can delay recovery in patients with whiplash (Björnstig et al., 1990; Bogduk and Yoganandan, 2001; Cassidy et al., 2000; Deans et al., 1986). According to available literature, chiropractic manipulation is commonly used, but rigorously controlled scientific studies are required to determine its effectiveness (Cassidy et al., 2000). There was no proven value for physiotherapy, although there were suggestions that it was beneficial in the short term. We recommend further exploration into the best strategies to educate the public health com munity about muscular and skeletal disorders worldwide.

Type of Head Restraint

The different head restraint types available across the current vehicle fleet include active, fixed or adjustable in the vertical direction only. We require more research on the traffic safety benefits of the three different types. It is generally agreed that the active and fixed restraints are usually more beneficial in light of the misuse of adjustable head restraints. A cost-benefit analysis should be conducted to investigate the difference in cost for active head restraints and costs for educational efforts to reduce misuse of adjustable head restraint systems. Are there reduced misuse rates reported in the fixed head restraint system? What is the comparative injury occurrence in the three different systems in rear end collisions? We require scientific guidelines for improved adjustment of different head restraint types to achieve optimum traffic safety benefits for drivers and occupants.

Protective in-Vehicle Equipment

The protective value of seat belts in whiplash is not clear, and there are no studies on the benefits and hazards of airbags or other automatic protection devices on whiplash. Laser-initiated braking systems can prevent collisions and intelligent seat design can halve the rate of neck injury if a collision occurs (Bannister et al., 2009). The efficacy of these devices requires further exploration.

Cost-Effectiveness

Future research should examine the best cost-effective mechanisms that the traffic safety community could utilize to change drivers' and occupants' safety behavior that enhances knowledge and attitudes of traffic safety benefits of the appropriate use of head restraints. Whiplash injuries constitute a huge proportion of insurance claims in many jurisdictions. Is there any reason for higher claim costs? What are the best possible ways that we could keep insurance claims down? Developments of new protection systems for rear end impacts should be a priority for the automotive industry. Not only active head restraint research, but also rear end collision avoidance technology must be adequately funded and developed. In addition, future research on whiplash injuries should be scientifically rigorous and could benefit from forming rational clinical and health care policies not only in highly motorized countries, but also in rapidly motorizing countries.

Cross-Disciplinary Initiatives

Epidemiological, real-world simulation, biomechanics and ergonomics research has proven itself a good source for generating correlational evidence related to rear end collisions and whiplash injuries. Building stronger links between whiplash injury epidemiology and neuroscience is also a valuable research strategy. This is especially important for exploring the biological plausibility of women and risk factors derived from existing studies. Cross-disciplinary projects between epidemiology and real-world simulation, bio mechanics, ergonomics and neuroscience may help us understand the pathways leading to whiplash injuries. The research concerning the epidemiology of whiplash has become more interesting and robust in recent years. Some new candidate exposures have been added to the list. Although some of these candidates will turn out to be false leads, we can expect that this list will continue to grow in the years to come. In light of the marked difference in biological vulnerability of women and men in whiplash injuries, further breakthroughs in research are imminent. Unlike biological risk factors, environmental risk factors will probably be of small effect on whiplash injury mechanisms, and will most likely vary considerably between demographic groups and the sexes. Regardless of these limitations, the clues that have been generated by the earlier research are too valuable to neglect. Future research should attempt to understand the risk of personal, social and environmental vulnerabilities in rear end collisions, head restraints and whiplash injuries.

Surveillance

Thatcham in the UK conducts research targeted at containing or reducing the cost of motor vehicle insurance claims, while maintaining standards of quality and safety. In the UK, the insurance industry handles a large volume of personal injury claims, but has poor understanding of the issues across industries and over time (Avery and Weekes, 2008). Under-reporting of minor injuries tends to occur because most collision databases require a police report or a tow–away, in order to be included in the database. A new approach was undertaken in gathering insurance personal injury claims data - Real World Injury Claims (RWIC) database. The objective of the database was to provide an improved understanding of the differing injuries seen in motor vehicle collisions and how vehicle design could be an influential factor (Avery and Weekes, 2008). The dataset provided a complete set of whiplash claims, without limiting inclusion, to allow a better understanding of these claims. Capturing the data in this way allowed for AIS coding of injuries and classification of whiplash injury according to the WAD scale (Avery and Weekes, 2008). The dataset includes assessment by an independent company of medical doctors, details of the collision impact and vehicles involved using a form completed by the patient, the emergency services, health services, and medical treatment provided, and an AIS and WAD score.

After analysing 4,000 claims, results showed that over 80% of injury claims were due to whiplash. Average recovery time was approximately 9 months, and 8% of whiplash injuries were deemed to be permanent injuries (Avery and

Weekes, 2008). Ninety-one percent of the claims were classified as WAD level 1 and the remaining 9% were level 2. Results were also positive with respect to changes in seat and head restraint design, such that whiplash injury claims were reduced in models that had incorporated anti-whiplash design (Avery and Weekes, 2008).

This novel database provides real-world evidence that there is a relationship between the vehicle model and the number of injury cases and encourages vehicle manufacturers to implement anti-whiplash design changes. This database could be a model for other countries to follow for their insurance databases.

Occupational Medicine

Physician specialists in occupational and environmental medicine are interested in neck pain from a broad perspective that ranges from primary prevention, to clinical care and the management of pain and disability. Occupational and environmental medicine (OEM), is both a clinical and preventive health specialty devoted to the prevention and management of occupational and environmental injury, illness and disability, and the promotion of the health and productivity of workers. Reflecting this dual preventive and clinical role, specialty training in occupational and environmental medicine includes epidemiology, biostatistics and ergonomics, as well as a focus on clinical care for and disability management, especially for musculoskeletal disorders (McCunney et al., 2003).

This broad scope of activities gives occupation and environmental medicine a more comprehensive focus than many other disciplines when addressing challenging public health issues, such as the prevention of neck pain and associated disability. In workplace settings, occupational medicine physicians work in collaboration with occupational health nurses, kinesiologists, ergonomists, industrial hygienists, safety specialists and human resource professionals in the identification, assessment and control of physical hazards in the workplace and general environment, and in helping to maintain the health and productivity of the workers.

Occupational and environmental medicine as a specialty has also assumed a leadership role in the use of evidence-based medicine (EBM) and effective disability management in workers' compensation settings. The American College of Occupational and Environmental Medicine (ACOEM), the primary professional organization for occupational and environmental medicine physicians, is in the development of evidence-based clinical practice guidelines for musculoskeletal disorders in working age adults. Such guidelines provide a reliable basis for clinical assessment and treatment of neck pain, using best scientific evidence, and incorporate a general approach based on rapid return to function and prevention of disability. In the US, the ACOEM guidelines have been adopted in whole or in part by several large health care systems, insurers, and state workers' compensation agencies (including those in California and New York) as the required (or "presumptively correct") guidelines for clinical care of musculoskeletal disorders. Health economics analysis suggests that when clinicians are required to follow comprehensive clinical practice guidelines and in workers' compensation settings, both medical costs and disability can be reduced.

BURDEN OF NECK PAIN IN OCCUPATIONAL SETTINGS

Historically, workers' compensation boards (WCB) and occupational health professionals in North America appear to have viewed neck pain as a relatively low priority, with WCBs reporting that neck pain accounts for less than 5% of lost-time claims. From both a research and clinical care perspective, literature on neck pain in workers has typically looked at neck pain associated with either back pain or upper limb disorders, or in relation to postural issues at work or related to ergonomic design of office furniture. In addition, in the past, there was a lack of easily identifiable evidence-based systematic literature reviews and clinical practice guidelines focused on neck pain prevention, diagnosis and treatment. This may have contributed to lack of awareness, interest and action.

Recent research has found that neck pain may account for a much larger burden of illness in working populations than originally thought. Cote and colleagues (2008), in a large cohort study investigating the prevalence and incidence of work absenteeism involving neck pain in workers in the province of Ontario, Canada, concluded that the WCB estimates of neck pain based on claims data grossly underestimates the burden of neck pain due to errors or limitations in administrative coding processes. Using codes specific for neck pain, the estimated percentage of lost-time claimants with neck pain in 1998 was 2.8% (95% CI 2.5–3.3), when they accounted for neck pain in workers coded with other injuries, the annual prevalence of neck pain increased to 11.3% (95% CI 9.5–13.1). Specifically they found that the number of lost-time claimants with soft-tissue disorders to the neck varied from 88% in those coded with a disorder of the neck region, to 69% for claimants coded with disorders of the back and 55% for claimants with a brain injury (concussion). This 403% difference suggests that a significant amount of neck pain is hidden within the classification system used to code claims. There was no data reported on number of lost-time claims attributed to motor vehicle collisions alone.

Studies that are focused on specific industries have noted a substantial rate of injury claims for neck pain related to motor vehicle collisions in the course of work activities. For instance, Fordyce in a study of neck injuries among electric utility workers over a 12-year period (from 1995-2007) found meter readers had the highest rate of neck injuries from motor vehicle collisions (22.8 per 10,000 employee-years), which was much higher than the rate of line workers (6.47 per 10,000 employee years) which was the job class with the next highest rate of neck injury from vehicular collisions (Fordyce et al., 2008).

A search of the literature has determined that there is a lack of research in the area of whiplash in occupational drivers, such as bus drivers, delivery persons, taxi drivers, etc. It is suggested that research be conducted to improve our understanding of whiplash and WAD in the occupational driver population, and to explore the differences from the general population.

From a societal perspective, whether a motor vehicle collision occurred at work, travelling to and from work, or at leisure, the total physical and socioeconomic burden of neck pain and disability to employers, employees, communities and families is substantial. From an employer perspective, the prevention of neck pain and disability through the appropriate use of head restraints and other collision avoidance systems could make a major contribution to enhancing workplace health and productivity. There is an extensive body of research demonstrating that the total cost to an employer due to an employee with a functionally limiting health problem, such as neck pain, includes not only the direct cost of medical care and salary replacement, but also indirect costs from productivity loss for that employee. While the direct costs (for medical care and salary replacement) can in themselves be substantial, the indirect costs in terms of lost productivity to the business are often 3 to 4 times higher than the direct costs. This underscores the importance for both employers and society in preventing neck pain episodes, and a rapid return to function for those who do develop neck problems (Loeppke et al., 2007; 2009).

Growing Corporate Responsibility to Ensure Employee Safety

From a regulatory perspective all employers have a responsibility to protect workers in the workplace including employees who use vehicles for work. Fleet owners and operators have the difficult task of addressing competing pressures from government and corporate demands including reducing pollution, cost of purchase or lease, and repair, among others (Fleet News, 2008). Until recently, purchasing vehicles with head restraints rated "good" were limited to higher end vehicles; however, this is no longer the case. The larger issue is the lack of awareness of fleet managers and employers to include head restraint ratings in their purchase or lease criteria.

NEED FOR KNOWLEDGE MOBILIZATION

There is typically a 15 – 20 year gap between research and its utilization to inform training, policy renewal and practice. The organizers[1] for the 2008 World Congress on Neck Pain strategically invited government agencies, research funding organizations, professional and licensing bodies to become congress sponsors and, if appropriate, to recommend scientific representatives to participate as members of the Scientific Review Committee with the goal of cultivating interest in post-congress dissemination and uptake (White et al., 2008). Following the world congress, key sponsors participated in a dissemination meeting hosted by the National Institute for Occupational Safety and Health to begin discussions on future activities and stimulate a "Call for Action".

CURRENT INITIATIVES

The Canadian Institute for the Relief of Pain and Disability (CIRPD) [2] as the lead organizer for the 2008 World Congress on Neck Pain is continuing its role in post-congress dissemination. To this end, it has partnered with the Canadian Institutes for Health Research (CIHR) and the CIHR Institute for Musculoskeletal Health and Arthritis under its Small Health Organization Partnership Program and The AUTO21 Network of Centres of Excellence[3] to fund Masters and Doctoral Awards focused on preventing and mitigating injuries arising from motor vehicle

---

[1] The World Congress on Neck Pain was organized by the Canadian Institute for the Relief of Pain and Disability in collaboration with the American College of Occupational and Environmental Medicine.

[2] CIRPD is a registered charity headquartered in Vancouver, Canada. Its mission is to reduce pain, pain suffering and disability by reducing the gap between research and practice.

[3] AUTO21 is Canada's national automotive research and development program supporting more than 300 Canadian researchers at 43 universities. More information can be found at www.auto21.ca.

collisions. In addition, it is working with licensing, professional and government bodies in the US and Canada to collaborate on translating research to practice initiatives.

The American College of Occupational and Environmental Medicine is updating clinical practice guidelines on neck pain which will incorporate new evidence based knowledge on clinical care and prevention.

AUTO21, one of the congress sponsors, recently funded a research project entitled, *Reducing Occupant Injury from Rear End Collisions* (Principal Investigator - Douglas Romilly, University of British Columbia) to: 1) develop new strategies to better implement existing knowledge about head restraints into practice, 2) develop new knowledge and technology to a) remove the role of the operator from the safety system and b) to enhance occupant protection through the design of future vehicle/occupant integrated active whiplash mitigation systems.

Future Directions from an Occupational Health Perspective

There is a need to create persuasive educational resources to educate all stakeholders responsible for occupational health and safety to:

1) Understand the scope of the problem
   a) prevalence of vehicle collisions and injuries,
   b) health, social and economic impact
   c) potential for prevention - on reducing injuries and related disability
   d) potential for prevention - economic modeling of injury prevention efforts

2) Prevention strategies – role of vehicle design in collision and injury prevention

   e) safety ratings from the Insurance Institute for Highway Safety (IIHS), including performance of head restraints, and collision safety features
   f) seat assessment tools from Insurance Corporation of British Columbia (ICBC),
   g) vehicle design elements that contribute to passenger safety
   h) tool kits for vehicle purchase selection focused on safety

3) Prevention strategies – shaping driving
   i) promotion of safe driving behaviors

j) tool kits for the family – creating safer drivers and occupants
k) tool kits for the community and schools – creating safer drivers and occupants
l) tool kits for the employers – creating safer drivers and occupants

4) Prevention strategies – promoting optimal recovery and reducing disability
   m) optimal evidence-based health care for injuries from vehicular collisions
   n) proactive management of disability to promote return to function

These future directions combined with a multi-faceted social marketing campaign would greatly benefit the population.

USING THE THREE ES OF INJURY PREVENTION

A variety of injury prevention efforts have proved effective and they involve three main strategies: engineering, education, and enforcement.

Many existing motor vehicles have adjustable head restraints, yet the literature reports high rates of misuse of this type of head restraint. A possibility exists to educate the public to achieve the safety benefits that the correct adjustment of head restraints would provide. Simultaneously, there is a clear need for advocating change and disseminating information to drivers, occupants, the health care community and policy makers. There are efforts to install active head restraints in new vehicles; however vehicles with fixed and adjustable head restraints will continue to be part of the existing vehicle fleet for considerable time in the future. We require a global effective education campaign that would enhance drivers' and occupants' knowledge about the traffic safety benefits of the correct adjustment of head restraints. An international organization that manages and advocates for injury prevention such as the World Health Organization (WHO), is a platform that could be utilized to convey the safety message to a broader audience of drivers and occupants worldwide. We therefore urge policy makers to promote this strategy by mobilizing resources, use the services of health personnel and transport policy makers around the world to convey the message that the correct adjustment of head restraints can prevent whiplash injuries.

Motor vehicle collision prevention is dependent on evidence-based interventions such as engineering to build road infrastructure, traffic law enforcement, driver licensing renewal policies, availability of driver education and training, increased awareness via evidence-based approaches to increase the proper use of vehicle safety equipment such as head restraints, seat belts and child safety seats. These are all strategies that support driver safety and reduce the burden of traffic-related injury in society; however, these strategies vary by country and jurisdiction. There are several promising strategies that would extensively benefit drivers, including: developing a safe road system through evidence-based engineering, enhancing crashworthiness of vehicles and increasing awareness of safety values of appropriate adjustment of seat belts, head restraints and child safety seats (Desapriya et al., 2006).

It is acknowledged that traffic law enforcement is one of the chief strategies in which many countries make heavy investments to reduce motor vehicle collisions. Enforcement initiatives could involve the police or community groups. However, driver education to enhance the understanding of safety values of existing safety equipment such as head restraints, safety belts and child safety seats is poor. This is evident by the higher incorrect adjustment of head restraints, lower use rates of seat belts and higher rates of misuse of child safety seats worldwide (Desapriya et al., 2008).

Approaches that incorporate education, engineering and enforcement to increase driver awareness around motor vehicle collision risk factors have been widely utilized to prevent collisions in many countries. Interventions such as media campaigns to increase driver awareness and education to reduce alcohol impaired driving and increase the use of seat belts and proper use of child restraint seats, were shown to be effective. It is recommended that effective principles and tools should be utilized to prevent future whiplash injuries. Lack of education or knowledge about the effectiveness of this intervention may hinder drivers' and occupants' motivation to properly adjust their head restraint, which will mitigate or prevent whiplash injuries in our communities.

The Social Marketing Approach

To increase awareness and enhance safety behavior to prevent whiplash injuries and associated disorders, behavior change at the population level is required. There are various tools that can be used to influence and change behavior. Education is a tool that is widely used, yet several education campaigns may be missing a crucial aspect that social marketing is able to provide. Education involves conveying messages to an audience informing them how we would like them to behave – *"don't drink and drive"*. Social marketing attempts to understand why an individual behaves in a certain way and appeals to personal benefits and alternate choices - *"don't drive and we will give you a ride home."*

To address behavioral issues related to the use of head restraints using social marketing, there is a need to adopt an innovative and engaging strategy. However, it is important to note that social marketing facilitates and incorporates the other foundational pillars of prevention, and success in reducing whiplash injuries will be garnered by the use of all three Es of injury prevention: *Education, Enforcement and Engineering.*

The following section discusses social marketing in terms of one of the pillars – *Education.* Public health professionals can consider using this strategic approach to educate the public about prevention of whiplash injuries whether it relates to awareness of the causes and severity of the issue, the recommended best practices for head restraint use, or driver and passenger awareness, attitudes and behaviors related to head restraint use.

Social marketing has been defined as a systematic application of marketing alongside other concepts and techniques to achieve specific behavioral goals for a social or public good (French and Blair-Stevens, 2006). The term social marketing was introduced in 1971 by Philip Kotler, a professor of management at Northwestern University. Earlier, in the 1960s it was described as commercial marketing in the public sector. Over time, social marketing has evolved and continues to progress. It is an evidence-based, dynamic and strategic approach for achieving and sustaining beneficial behavior change.

Social marketing is also considered a powerful knowledge translation tool that draws from a wide variety of theory and practice and uses best practices to raise awareness and eventually influence attitudes and behaviors.

How is social marketing different from health education?

Social Marketing is…	Social Marketing is not…
About social or behavior change	Just advertising
Targeting a given population at risk	Reaching everyone through a media blitz
Strategic and efficient use of resources	An image campaign, done in a vacuum
Integrated with a long-term plan	A magic bullet

Social marketing uses a combination of marketing and health communication techniques to achieve social good or targeted behavior goals. Social marketing focuses on a target population and is developed to provide messages that are intended to motivate a desired behavior through revealing various choices and their risks and benefits. It takes into consideration the broader determinants of health and develops campaign concepts based on an understanding of the context in which the target audience exists (e.g. SES, education, age, sex).

Why Use Social Marketing in Public Health?

Social marketing campaigns have shown success in improving health-related knowledge, awareness and behaviors (Banspach, 2008; Grier and Bryant, 2005). They provide a relatively new perspective to health and safety promotion, and challenge health professionals to think and plan strategies using target audience and market research. Studies have shown that a well-tested and strategically planned social marketing campaign that is based on well-supported behavioral theories (e.g. Stages of Change Model – Prochaska and DiClemente, 1983) can work to bring about behavior change. However, it is crucial to realize that behavior change is a complex process and may take years to achieve. This approach, however, demands that health professionals develop or include expertise about understanding their target audience's current behaviors and readiness to change, prior to developing a campaign. Table 4 illustrates stages of readiness that help to understand the target audience's readiness to change.

Table 4. Stages of Change Model

Pre-contemplation	Not even thinking about it – not aware of whiplash injuries
Contemplation	Thinking about it - have heard about whiplash injuries but are not quite motivated to take preventative measures
Preparation	Planning to act – Are aware of the risks and consequences of whiplash injuries. They are aware that by adjusting head restraints, these injuries can be prevented
Action	Make a move but not yet a habit – Adjust head restraints before driving to minimize risk for whiplash injuries
Maintenance	Example- Always adjust head restraint before driving

Principles of Social Marketing

Figure 2 demonstrates the principles of social marketing indicating that it revolves around the target audience (also referred to as the consumer, customer or public). It emphasizes the importance of consumer and market research. It encourages social marketers to consider a theoretical framework (e.g. behavior change model) to understand the target audience's current behaviors and gain insight to consumers' thoughts, beliefs, fears, and motivations around the desired behavior. This insight may be garnered through the use of surveys, interviews, focus groups or observational studies.

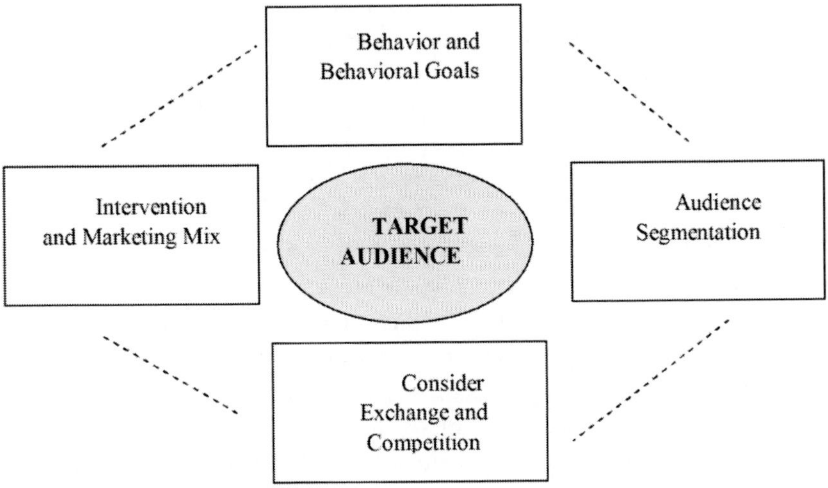

Figure 2. The Principles of Social Marketing.

Social marketing puts a strong emphasis on understanding the context in which the target audience exists, and in which the desired behavior is to be performed. It requires understanding of the competing interests, factors and barriers facing the target audience in attempting to implement the desired behavior. And, it recommends that program planners consider the value, and incentives necessary for the target audience to adopt the desired behavior.

Social marketing uses the concepts of competition to examine the factors that compete for people's attention and willingness or ability to adopt a desired behavior. Furthermore, social marketing puts a strong emphasis on understanding what is to be offered to the target audience, based upon what they value and consider important (National Social Marketing Centre; NSMC-UK).

Target audience segmentation is a fundamental part of social marketing. It is a process of examining the target audience and seeking to identify distinct sub-groups (segments) that may have similar needs, attitudes or behaviors. This approach helps in understanding the current level of knowledge, stage of behavior and readiness for change for a given target audience and ensures a straightforward measure of success for the campaign outcomes.

The social marketing approach is dynamic and uses multiple channels and interventions to convey messages. This diverse approach is referred to as 'marketing mix'. This approach helps to engage the target audience, empowers them with choices and can lead toward initiating a social movement. Social marketing has been effective in bringing about changes in health-related behaviors and creating significant social change. An example of this is the national tobacco control campaign in England (National Tobacco Control Campaign, UK). The previous success of social marketing to improve health behaviors provides impetus to consider its utility to influence the correct use of head restraints among drivers and passengers. A social marketing campaign to reduce whiplash injuries through increased correct use of head restraints while driving would need to:

1) Determine the target audience – e.g. whiplash injury statistics to determine the audience or audience segment to target
2) Understand the context in which the target audience exists – e.g. demographic data, vehicle use information
3) Understand the target audience's awareness, current attitude and knowledge of the whiplash injury issue
4) Understand the competing factors – e.g. convenience, time consumption, speed
5) Understand what is important and motivates the target audience – what positive benefits could be considered that would resonate with the target population and that would motivate and lead to a change in behavior to correct head restraint use
6) Understand the value and incentives that would cause and maintain correct use of head restraints
7) Develop, test and refine marketing campaign messages and communication vehicles
8) Launch and monitor the campaign

Examples of Successful Social Marketing Campaigns related to Driving

Click It or Ticket (North Carolina, US)

This campaign began in 1993 and is ongoing. The target audience included drivers and passengers with the goal of increasing seatbelt use. The outcomes included an increase in seatbelt use from 63% to 80% in North Carolina. There was also a 14% reduction in fatal and serious highway injuries. The campaign concepts and activities were developed based on social marketing principles including marketing mix, community outreach and enforcement, audience segmentation, and redefined benefits based on consumer analysis. The details of this campaign are available at: http://www.social-marketing.org/success/cs-clickit.html.

Copy Cat (UK)

This campaign ran for 1 year from 2007-2008 and targeted parents of 4-11 year old children.

The goal of the campaign was to increase seatbelt use in parents so that children would copy this behavior.

The outcomes demonstrated that 40% of the sample was aware of the Copy Cat campaign in the first year and 75% realized that the advertising conveyed the concept that children copy parents' behavior.

The campaign concepts and strategies were developed based on consumer insight and audience segmentation. The details of the campaign are available at: http://www.larsoa.org.uk/news.php?article_id=386.

Zero Tolerance Means Zero Chances (US)

The results of this campaign demonstrated that awareness of the no tolerance law rose from 61% to 63% over six months. The details of the campaign are available at: http://www.nhtsa.dot.gov/people/injury/alcohol/zeropr/index.html.

Friends Don't Let Friends Drive Drunk (US)

The outcomes of this campaign were positive showing that 80% of the sample reported that they took action to stop a friend from driving. Twenty-five percent of the sample actually did stop a friend from driving while intoxicated. The details of the campaign are available at: http://www.adcouncil.org/default.aspx?id=137.

Age 4 to 9? It's Booster Seat Time! (Canada)

This Canadian media campaign nearly doubled child booster seat use from 24% to 47% in the geographical areas that received the campaign (Howard et al., 2006). However, it should be noted that this occurred without significant gains in general booster seat knowledge (Howard et al., 2006).

Back Pain: Don't Take It Lying Down (Australia)

From 1997 to 1999, a campaign ran in Victoria, Australia for workers. It was named 'Back Pain: Don't Take it Lying Down'. This mass media campaign was successful in enhancing Victorian workers' self-management abilities, thus and changing attitudes and behaviour concerning back pain (Buchbinder, 2008).

The Australian study (Buchbinder and Jolley, 2004; Buchbinder et al., 2001) used prime-time television advertisements that featured health professionals, sports and local television celebrities, at the cost of 10.1 million dollars over three years, had the largest impact showing dramatic changes in beliefs about back pain as a consequence of advertising in the general population and general practitioners. The advertisements contributed to a 15% reduction in back pain claims during the intervention period and a 20% reduction in medical costs. Variations of the Australian study were attempted in Norway, Scotland and Alberta with much lower investment. The Alberta study invested less approximately 1 million dollars over three years, Norway less than $500,000 (Scottish figures not available). These interventions delivered fewer messages and did not use prime time television resulting in much lower market penetration. There were modest though significant changes in beliefs and attitudes in Norway and Scotland, and no impact on work absences, or back pain claims.

Drive safely – Avoid Accidents – Prevent Consequences of Accidents (Sweden)

The Swiss Insurance Association in collaboration with the Council for Accident Prevention and the Swiss Road Safety Fund commenced a prevention campaign to increase awareness of the correct headrestraint position for safety (Soltermann, 2007). The campaign motto is 'Drive safely – Avoid accidents – Prevent consequences of accidents'. Results of this campaign have not yet been published. A series of short commercials and posters can be found at http://www.kopfstuetzen.ch/

Neck Pain Beliefs and Head Restraint Social Marketing Campaigns

Bostick and colleagues (2007) conducted a population-based cross-sectional study surveying beliefs about neck pain from whiplash injury, work-related neck pain, and work-related upper extremity pain in two Canadian provinces to capture baseline data as well as explore whether the use of a social marketing campaign might be warranted. He found that the majority of respondents agreed that staying active was more important than rest which is congruent with evidence-based guidelines, however they found a much higher level of pessimism regarding likelihood of recovery of neck pain arising from motor vehicle collisions within the population. This higher level of pessimism concerning whiplash recovery might be an important consideration in developing and testing social marketing messages, for instance, "Worried about Whiplash?–Did you know Prevention is Possible?"

Social marketing campaigns can be effective means of influencing attitudes and behaviors, however they require sufficient investment in planning, implementation and evaluation. We believe such investment is warranted.

CONCLUSION

This book has provided a summary of the past, present and future of the relationship between head restraints and whiplash injuries. We have examined the evolution of head restraints, the scientific evidence, the technological advances and the legislation and ratings surrounding their efficacy. With respect to preventing whiplash injury, it is evident that the engineering (technology) has advanced with the addition of active head restraints. The legislative side of enforcement has also advanced with the future implementation of a global technical regulation surrounding head restraints. We are aware that police enforcement of the proper position of an adjustable head restraint is not feasible. Educational efforts have been limited and untargeted. We recognize the complexity of the issue, yet changing the population's behavior is the final required step. A social marketing campaign to address the issue would be beneficial for the prevention of whiplash and related injuries.

We end by reiterating the closing remarks of Professor Matthew H. Liang, the Scientific Chair at the 2008 World Congress on Neck Pain.

> From a public health perspective the best way to reduce individual suffering and the socio-economic burden of neck pain arising from motor vehicle collisions is for the public to use vehicles with good head restraints and to make sure that head restraints be adjusted appropriately.

ACKNOWLEDGEMENTS

We would like to acknowledge Dr. Sayed Subzwari, (International Medical Graduate-Centre for Community Child Health Research, BC Injury Research and Prevention Unit) for his involvement in the initial planning of the book. We would like to thank Doug Romilly for his assistance and expert advice, as well as David Zuby (Insurance Institute for Highway Safety), Jocelyn Pedder (RONA Kinetics), and Matthew Avery (THATCHAM, UK) for historical notes.

REFERENCES

Acar, M; Clark, SJ; Crouch, R. Smart head restraint system. *International Journal of Crashworthiness,* 2007, 12, 429-435.

Ad Hoc Group on Head Restraints. European Commision. Meeting Minutes, Brussels, 23 June 2006.

Aker, PD; Gross, AR; Goldsmith, CH; Peloso, P. Conservative management of mechanical neck pain: systematic overview and meta-analysis. *British Medical Journal,* 1996, 313, 1291–1296.

Allen, MJ; Barnes, MR; Bodivala, GG. The effect of seatbelt legislation on injuries sustained by car occupants. *Injury*, 1985, 16, 471.

Arbabi, S; Wahl, WL; Hemmila, MR; Kohoyda-Inglis, C; Taheri, PA; Wang, SC. The cushion effect. *Journal of Trauma,* 2003, 54(6), 1090-1093.

Ardoino, PL. Kinematics and dynamics of the vehicle/seat/occupant/system regarding whiplash injuries. In: Cesarani, A, Alpini, D, Bonvier, R, et al., editors. *Whiplash Injuries: Diagnosis and Treatment.* Berlin: Springer; 1996.

Avery, M. An International insurance protocol for dynamic testing of vehicle seats to reduce whiplash injury risk. *Proceedings of the World Congress on Neck Pain,* January 20-22, 2008, Los Angeles, CA, pp 83.

Avery, M; Giblen, E; Weekes, A; Zuby, D. Developments in dynamic whiplash assessment procedures. *Proceedings International Conference on Neck Injuries in Road Traffic and Prevention Strategies.* Munich, Germany, 2007, Paper No. 5, pp 14.

Avery, M; Weekes, A. Real world injury claims database: a new approach in gathering insurance personal injury claims data. *Proceedings of the World Congress on Neck Pain*, January 20-22, 2008, Los Angeles, CA, pp 84-85.

Banks, R; Martini, J; Smith, H; Bowels, A; Mcnish, T; Howard, R. Alignment of the lumbar vertebrae in a driving posture. *Journal of Crash Prevention and Injury Control,* 2000, 2(2),123-130.

Bannister, G; Amirfeyz, R; Kelley, S; Gargan, M. Whiplash injury. *Journal of Bone and Joint Surgery British Volume,* 2009, 91(7), 845-850.

Banspach, SW. The VERB™ Campaign. *American Journal of Preventive Medicine,* 2008, 34(6), S275.

Berglund, A; Alfredsson, L; Jensen, I; Bodin, L; Nygren, A. Occupant- and crash-related factors associated with the risk of whiplash injury. *Annals of Epidemiology,* 2003, 13(1), 66-72.

Björnstig, U; Hildingsson, C; Toolanen, G. Soft-tissue injury of the neck in a hospital based material. *Scandinavian Journal of Social Medicine,* 1990, 18(4), 263-267.

Bogduk, N; Marsland, A. The cervical zygapophyseal joints as a source of neck pain. *Spine,* 1988, 13, 610-617.

Bogduk, N; Yoganandan, N. Biomechanics of the cervical spine. Part 3: minor injuries. *Clinical Biomechanics,* 2001, 16, 267–275.

Borchgrevink, GE; Lereim, I; Royneland, L; Bjorndal, A; Haraldseth, O. National health insurance consumption and chronic symptoms following mild neck sprain injuries in car accidents. *Scand J. Soc. Med.,* 1996, 24(4), 264-271.

Bostick, GP; Ferrari, R; Carroll, LJ; et al. A population-based survey of beliefs about neck pain from whiplash injury, work-related neck pain, and work-related upper extremity pain. *European Journal of Pain,* 2008, in press.

Bostrom, O; Haland, Y; Lovsund, P; Svensson, MY. Neck injury criterion (NIC) and its relevance to various possible neck injury mechanisms. In: Yoganandan N, Pintar FA (eds). *Frontiers in Whiplash Trauma: Clinical and Biomechanical.* The Netherlands: IOS Press; 2000; 455-466.

Bostrom, O; Krafft, M; Aldman, B; et al. Prediction of neck injuries in rear impacts based on accident data and simulations. *Proceedings International IRCOBI Conference on the Biomechanics of Impacts,* September 24-26, 1997, Hannover, Germany, pp 251-264.

Boulanger, BR; Rodriguez, A. Body habitus as a predictor of injury pattern after blunt trauma. *J. Trauma,* 1992, 33(2), 228-232.

Braddick, MR; Love, G. Car head restraints. *BMJ,* 1990, 301, 440.

Brown, B; Nepomuceno, J. A review of educational strategies to mitigate soft-tissue neck injuries. *Proceedings Whiplash Associated Disorders World Congress* (Traffic Safety and Auto Engineering Session), February 1999, Vancouver, BC, pp 489-499.

Buchbinder, R. Optimizing care for people with chronic disease. Self-management education en masse: effectiveness of the Back Pain: Don't take it lying down mass media campaign. *Medical Journal of Australia*, 2008, 189(10 Suppl.), S29-S32.

Buchbinder, R; Jolley, D. Population based intervention to change back pain beliefs: three year follow up population survey. *BMJ,* 2004, 328, 321.

Buchbinder, R; Jolley, D; Wyatt, M. Population based intervention to change back pain beliefs and disability: three part evaluation. *BMJ,* 2001, 322, 1516-1520.

Buitenhuis, J; de Jong, PJ; Jaspers, JP; Groothoff, JW. Work disability after whiplash: a prospective cohort study. *Spine*, 2009, 1, 34(3), 262-267.

Caddy, J. Risk factors for 'whiplash' in drivers: a cohort study of rear-end traffic crashes. *Injury,* 1998, 29(2), 147.

Carlsson, G; Nilsson, S; Nilsson-Ehle, A; et al. Neck injuries in rear-end car collisions: Biomechanical considerations to improve head restraints. *Proceedings of the International IRCOBI/AAAM Conference on the Biomechanics of Impacts,* Göteborg, Sweden, 1995, 277-289.

Cassidy, JD; Carroll, LJ; Côté, P; Lemstra, M; Berglund, A; Nygren, A. Effect of eliminating compensation for pain and suffering on the outcome of insurance claims for whiplash injury. *New England Journal of Medicine,* 2000, 20, 342(16), 1179-1186.

Chapline, J; Ferguson, SA; Lillis, RP; Lund, AK; Williams, AF. Neck pain and head restraint position relative to the driver's head in rear-end collisions. *Accident Analysis and Prevention,* 2000, 32, 287–297.

Cote, P; van der Velde, G; Cassidy, JD; et al. The burden and determinants of neck pain in workers. Results of The Bone and Joint Decade 2000-2010 Task Force on Neck Pain and Its Associated Disorders. *Spine,* 2008, 33(4S), S60-S74.

Croft, AC; Haneline, MT; Freeman, MD. Low speed frontal crashes and low speed rear crashes: Is there a differential risk for injury? *Annual Proceedings – Association for the Advancement of Automotive Medicine,* 2002, 46, 79–91.

Cullen, E; Stabler, KM; Mackay, GM; Parkin, S. Head restraint positioning and occupant safety in rear impacts: the case for smart restraints. *Proceedings of the 1996 International Conference on the Biomechanics of Impacts, IRCOBI,* Lyon, France, pp. 137–152.

Darok, M; Leinzinger, EP; Eichberger, A; Steffan, H. Neck injury criterion validation using human subjects and dummies. In: Yoganandan N, Pintar FA (eds). *Frontiers in Whiplash Trauma: Clinical and Biomechanical.* The Netherlands: IOS Press; 2000; 409-434.

Deans, GT; McGalliard, JN; Kerr, M; Rutherford, WH. Neck sprain-a major cause of disability following car accidents. *Injury,* 1987, 18, 10-12.

Deans, GT; McGalliard, JN; Rutherford, WH. Incidence and duration of neck pain among patients injured in car accidents. *BMJ (Clinical Research Edition),* 1986, 11, 292(6513), 94-95.

Deng, B. *Biomechanics of the human cadaver cervical spine during low speed read-end impacts.* Ph.D. Dissertation, Wayne State University, 1999.

Deng, B; Luan, F; Begeman, PC; Yang, KH; King, AI; Tashman, S. Testing shear hypothesis of whiplash injury using experimental and analytical approaches. In: Yoganandan N, Pintar FA (eds). *Frontiers in Whiplash Trauma: Clinical and Biomechanical.* The Netherlands: IOS Press; 2000a; 491-509.

Deng, B; Begeman, PC; Yang, KY; King, AI; Tashman, S. Kinematics of human cadaver cervical spine during low-speed rear-end impacts. *Stapp Car Crash Journal,* 2000b, 44, 171–188.

Department of Transport, Government of Canada. Regulations amending the motor vehicle safety regulations (head restraints). *Canada Gazette,* September 13, 2008,142(37).

DeRosia, J; Yoganandan, N. Lessons from stages rear-end collisions using human volunteers. In: Yoganandan N, Pintar FA (eds). *Frontiers in Whiplash Trauma: Clinical and Biomechanical.* The Netherlands: IOS Press; 2000, 265-294.

Desapriya, E; Pike, I; Subzwari, S. Traffic safety and sports utility vehicles. *Lancet,* 2006, 15, 368(9531), 201-202.

Desapriya, E; Fujiwara, T; Scime, G; Babul, S; Pike, I. Compulsory child restraint seat law and motor vehicle child occupant deaths and injuries in Japan 1994-2005. *International Journal of Injury Control and Safety Promotion,* 2008, 15(2), 93-97.

Dippel, C; Muser, MH; Walz, F; Niederer, P; Kaeser, R. Neck injury prevention in rear impact crashes. *Proceedings International IRCOBI Conference on the Biomechanics of Impacts,* September 24-26, 1997, Hannover, Germany, pp 239-250.

Dolinis, I. Risk factors for 'whiplash' in drivers: a cohort study of rear-end traffic crashes. *Injury,* 1997, 28(3), 173-179.

Dunn, EJ; Blazar, S. Soft-Tissue injuries of the lower cervical spine. *Instructional Course Lectures, American Academy Orthopaedic Surgeons,* Vol XXXVI, 499-512, 1987.

Edwards, M; Smith, S; Zuby, DS; Lund, AK. Improved seat and head restraint evaluations. *Proceedings 19th Enhanced Safety of Vehicles Conference,* 2005, Paper 05-0374-0.

Eichberger, A; Geigle, BC; Fachbach, B; Steffan, H; Hell, W; Langweider, K. Comparison of different car seats regarding head-neck kinematics of volunteers during rear end impact. *Proceedings International IRCOBI Conference on the Biomechanics of Impacts,* September 11-13, 1996, Dublin, Ireland, pp 153-164.

European Enhanced Vehicle-safety Committee (EEVC), WG 20 Report. *Updated state-of-the-art review on whiplash injury prevention.* March 2005, pp. 21.

European New Car Assessment Programme (Euro NCAP). (2008). Available from: http://www.euroncap.com/whiplash.aspx.

Evans, L. Safety-belt effectiveness: the influence of crash severity and selective recruitment. *Accid. Anal. Prev.,* 1996, 28(4), 423-433.

Evans, L; Frick, MC. Car size or car mass: which has greater influence on fatality risk? *American Journal of Public Health,* 1992, 82, 1105-1112.

Evans, L; Frick, MC. Mass ratio and relative driver fatality risk in two-vehicle crashes. *Accid Anal Prev,* 1993, 25, 213-224.

Farmer, CM; Wells, JK; Lund, AK. Effects of head restraint and seat redesign on neck injury risk in rear-end crashes. *Traffic Injury Prevention,* 2003, 4, 83-90.

Farmer, CM; Wells, JK; Werner, JV. Relationship of head restraint positioning to driver neck injury in rear-end crashes. *Accid. Anal. Prev.,* 1999, 31, 719-728.

Farmer, CM; Zuby, DS; Wells, JK; Hellinga, LA. Relationship of dynamic seat ratings to real-world neck injury rates. *Traf. Inj. Prev.,* 2008, 9, 561-567.

Federal Motor Vehicle Safety Standard 202a (FMVSS 202a), Head Restraints; Federal Register; US National Highway Traffic Safety Administration.

Fleet News. Safety dilemma for fleet operators. Friday May 2, 2008. Available from: http://www.fleetnews.co.uk/news/story/?nID=47136.

Fockler, SK; Vavrik, J; Kristiansen, L. Motivating drivers to correctly adjust head restraints: assessing effectiveness of three different interventions. *Accid. Anal. Prev.,* 1998, 30(6), 773-780.

Fordyce, T; Kelsh, M; Mezei, G. Neck injuries among electric utility workers: 1995-2005. *Proceedings World Congress on Neck Pain*, January 20-22, 2008, Los Angeles, CA, pp 95.

Foret-Bruno, JY; Dauvilliers, F; Tarriere, C. Influence of the seat and head rest stiffness on the risk of cervical injuries. *13th International Technical Conference on Experimental Safety Vehicles,* S-8-W-19, 968-974, 1991.

French, J; Blair-Stevens, C. *Social Marketing Pocket Guide* (1st Edition). National Social Marketing Centre for Excellence. Available from: http://www.nsms.org.uk.

Galasko, CS; Murray, PM; Pitcher, M. Neck sprains after road traffic accidents: a modern epidemic. *Injury,* 1993, 24, 155–157.

Gane, J. Measurement of vehicle head restraint geometry. SAE No. 1999-01-0639. In: *Occupant Protection* (SP-1432), pp 45-50, 1999.

Gane, J; Pedder, J. Head restraint measuring device. Paper No. 96-S10-W-27. 1996.

Garrett, JW; Morris, DF. Performance evaluation of automobile head restraints. SAE Warrendale, PA. Technical Paper #720034; 1972.

Gay, JR; Abbott, KH. Common whiplash injuries of the neck. *Journal of the American Medical Association,* 1953, 29, 152(18),1698–1704.

Geddes, E; Fockler, S; Felipe, E. Observational study of driver and passenger head restraint positions. *Proceedings of the CMRSC-X,* Toronto, Ontario, June 1997, pp 442-453.

Geigl, BC; Leinzinger, P; Roll; Muhlbauer, M; Bauer, G. The movement of the head and cervical spine during rear-end impact. *Proceedings 1994 International IROCOI Conference on the Biomechanics of Impacts,* September 21-23, 1994, Lyon, France, pp 127-137.

Gibson, T; McIntosh, A. Rear end impact associated neck injuries. *Proceedings of the 1997 Australian MADYMO Users Meeting,* Melbourne, April 1997.

Gotten, N. Survey of one hundred cases of whiplash injury after settlement of litigation. *JAMA*, 1956, 27, 162(9), 865–867.

Grier, S; Bryant, CA. Social marketing in public health. *Annual Review of Public Health,* 2005, 26, 319-339. Available from: http://www.toniyancey.com/ is19/110706a.pdf.

Gross, AR; Aker, PD; Goldsmith, CH; Peloso, P. Conservative management of mechanical neck disorders. A systematic overview and meta-analysis. *Journal of Current Clinical Trials,* 1996, 30, 200-201.

Gupta, V; Menon, R; Gupta, S; Mani, A; Shanmugavelu, I; Kossar, J. Improved occupant protection through advanced seat design. *Proceedings 15th International Technical Conference on Enhanced Safety of Vehicles,* May 13-16, 1996, Melbourne, Australia, pp 181-191.

Guzman, J; Haldeman, S; Carroll, LJ; et al. Clinical practice implications of the Bone and Joint Decade 2000-2010 Task Force on Neck Pain and Its Associated Disorders: From concepts and findings to recommendations. *Spine,* 2008, 15, 33(4S), S199-213.

Haland, Y; Lindh, F; Fredriksson, R; Svensson, M. The influence of the car body and the seat on the loading of the front seat occupant's neck in low speed rear impacts. *Proceedings 29th ISATA Conference,* June, 1996, Italy, pp 21-30.

Halping, J; Greenspan, AI; Haileyesus, T; Annest, JL. The effect of counting principal and secondary injuries on national estimates of motor vehicle-related trauma: a NEISS-AIP special study. *Inj. Prev.,* 2009, 15(5), 328-333.

Haneline, MT. The notion of a "whiplash culture": a review of the evidence. *J. Chiropr. Med.,* 2009, 8(3), 119-124.

Hartlieb, M; Bihler, E; Bretner, R; et al. NECK-PRO – Mercedes Benz Active Head Restraint. *Proceedings of the International Conference for Neck*

Injuries in Road Traffic and Prevention Strategies, November 5-6, 2007, Munich, Germany.

Hasegawa, T; Kudoh, T. Development of a test method to evaluate both stiffness and interaction of compatibility performance. *SAE International Journal of Passenger Cars-Mechanical Systems,* 2009, 1(1), 679-688.

Hayes, CW; Conway, WF; Walsh, JW; Coppage, L; Gerwin, AS. Seat belt injuries: radiological and clinical correlation. *RadioGraphics,* 1991, 11, 23-36.

Hell, W; Langwieder, K. Reported soft-tissue injuries after reat-end car collisions. *Proceedings International IRCOBI Conference on the Biomechanics of Impacts,* September 16-18, 1998, Goteborg, Sweden, pp 261-274.

Hijioka, A; Narusawa, K; Nakamura, T. Risk factors for long-term treatment of whiplash injury in Japan: analysis of 400 cases. *Archives of Orthopaedic and Trauma Surgery*, 2001, 121(9), 490-493.

Hildingsson, C; Toolanen, G. Outcome after soft-tissue injury of the cervical spine. A prospective study of 93 car-accident victims. *Acta Orthopaedica Scandinavica,* 1990, 61(4), 357-359.

Himmetoglu, S; Acar, M; Bouazza-Marouf, K; Taylor, AJ. Energy-absorbing car seat designs for reducing whiplash. *Traf. Inj. Prev.,* 2008, 9, 583-591.

Hogg-Johnson, S; van der Velde, G; Carroll, LJ; et al. The burden and determinants of neck pain the general population. Results of the Bone and Joint Decade 2000-2010 Task Force on Neck Pain and Its Associated Disorders. *Spine,* 2008, 33(4S), S39-S51.

Holm, LW; Carroll, LJ; Cassidy, D; et al. The burden and determinants of neck pain in whiplash-associated disorders after traffic collisions. Results of the Bone and Joint Decade 2000-2010 Task Force on Neck Pain and Its Associated Disorders. *Spine,* 2008, 33(4S), S52-S59.

Hong, SJ. Investigation of whiplash injury in Korea: Use of head restraint and its statistical analysis. *Proceedings of the JSAE Congress,* Japan, 2004, pp 21-24.

Hopkin, JM; Simpson, HF. Valuation of Road Accidents. Transport Research Laboratory (TRL) Report Number 163, Transport Research Laboratory UK, 1995.

Howard, A; Beben, N; Rothman, L; Fiissel, D; MacArthur, C. Evaluation of safe kids week 2004: age 4 to 9? It's booster seat time! *Inj. Prev.,* 2006, 12, 316-319.

Howard, RP; Bowles, AP; Guzman, HM; Krenrich, SW. Head, neck, and mandible dynamics generated by 'whiplash'. *Accid. Anal. Prev.,* 1998, 30(4), 525-534.

Huang, SC; Huston, RL. Influence of the head restraint position on dynamic response of the head/neck system under whiplash loading. *Biomed Eng. Appl. Basis. Comm.,* 2003, 15, 164-169.

Huelke, DF; Marsh, JC; DiMento, L; Sherman, HW; Ballard, WJ. Injury causation in rollover accidents. *Proceedings 17th American Association for Automotive Medicine Conference,* Morton Grove, IL, AAAM, 1973, pp 87-115.

Hurwitz, EL; Aker, PD; Adams, AH; Meeker, WC; Shekelle, PG. Manipulation and mobilization of the cervical spine: a systematic review of the literature. *Spine,* 1996, 21, 1746-1760.

Hynd, D; Carroll, JA; Bartlett, RS. UK cost-benefit analysis: enhanced geometric requirements for vehicle head restraints. Transport Research Laboratory (TRL) Transport Research Laboratory UK, 2008.

Hynes, LM; Dickey, JP. The rate of change of acceleration: implications to head kinematics during rear-end impact. *Accid. Anal. Prev.,* 2008, 40, 1063-1068.

Insurance Institute of Highway Safety (IIHS). Procedure for evaluating motor vehicle head restraints. March 2008; 3: pp 1. Available from: http://www.iihs.org/ratings/protocols/pdf/head_restraint_procedure.pdf.

IIHS. *Save our necks.* Insurance Institute for Highway Safety Status Report, 1999, 34(5).

IIHS. *Head restraints will be higher and closer to the back of the head.* Status Report, 2005, 40(2).

International Insurance Whiplash Prevention Group (IIWPG). *Rationale for IIWPG ratings of seats and head restraints for neck injury prevention.* December, 2004.

Jakobsson, L. Field analysis of AIS 1 neck injuries in rear-end car impacts -injury reducing effect of the WHIPS seat. *Journal of Whiplash Related Disorders,* 2005, 3(2), 37–53.

Jakobsson, L; Isaksson-Hellman, I; Lindman, M. WHIPS (Volvo cars' whiplash protection system) - The development and real world performance of WHIPS. *Traf Inj Prev,* 2008, 9, 600-605.

Jakobssen, L; Lundell, B; Norin, H; Isaksson-Hellman, I. WHIPS – Volvo's whiplash protection study. *Proceedings Whiplash Associated Disorders World Congress (Traffic Safety and Auto Engineering Session),* February 1999, Vancouver, BC, pp 521-536.

Jakobsson, L; Lundell, H; Norin, H; Isaksson-Hellman, I. WHIPS-Volvo's whiplash protection study. *Accid. Anal. Prev.,* 2000a, 32, 307-319.

Jakobsson, L; Norin, H. AIS1 neck injury reducing effect of WHIPS (Whiplash Protection System). *Proceedings of International IRCOBI Conference on the Biomechanics of Impacts,* 2004, Graz, Austria, pp 297-305.

Jakobsson, L; Norin, H; Svensson, MY. Parameters influencing AIS 1 neck injury outcome in frontal impacts. *Traf. Inj. Prev.,* 2004, 5, 156–163.

Jakobsson, L; Norin, H; Isaksson-Hellman, I. Parameters influencing the risk of AIS1 neck injuries in frontal and side impacts. *Proceedings of the International Research Council on the Biomechanics of Impact (IRCOBI),* Montpellier, France, September 20-22, 2000b.

Jakobsson, L; Norin, H; Jernstrom, C; Svensson, SE; Iasksson-Hellman, I; Svensson, MY. Analysis of different head and neck responses in rear-end car collisions using a new human-like mathematical model. *Proceedings International IRCOBI Conference on the Biomechanics of Impacts,* September 8-10, 1993, Einhoven, The Netherlands, pp 109-125.

Johnson, D. Counseling to reduce road injuries and deaths. *Canadian Family Physician,* 1996, 42, 2154-2158.

Jonsson, B; Svensson, MY; Linder, A; Bjornstig, U. BioRID II manikin and human seating position in relation to car head restraint. *International Journal of Crashworthiness,* 2008, 13, 479-485.

Kahane, CJ. An evaluation of head restraints, Federal Motor Vehicle Safety Standard 202. Report no. DOT-HS-806-108. Washington DC: US Department of Transportation; 1982.

Kallieris, D; Mattern, R; Miltner, E; et al. Considerations for a neck injury criterion. SAE 912916. *Proceedings of the 35th Stapp Car Crash Conference,* Detroit, MI, Society of Automotive Engineers, 1991, 401-415.

Khan, S; Bannister, G; Gargan, M; Asopa, V; Edward, A. Prognosis following a second whiplash injury. *Injury,* 2000, 31, 249-251.

Kihlberg, JK. Flexion-torsion neck injury in rear impacts. *Proceedings of the 13th Annual Conference of the American Association for Automotive Medicine*, Ann Arbor, Michigan, 1969, pp 1-16.

Kim, A; Prasad, P. Hybrid III and Hybrid III with a TRID neck in low-speed rear impacts. In: Yoganandan N, Pintar FA (eds). *Frontiers in Whiplash Trauma: Clinical and Biomechanical.* The Netherlands: IOS Press; 2000; 435-454.

Kitagawa, Y; Yasuki, T; Hasegawa, J. Research study on neck injury lessening with active head restraint using human body FE model. *Traf. Inj. Prev.,* 2008, 9, 574-582.

Kivioja, J. *Patient related aspects on WAD.* Stockholm, Sweden: Karolinska University Press; 2004.

Kleinberger, M; Sun, E; Saunders, J; Zhou, Z. Effects of head restraint position on neck injury in rear impact. *Proceedings Whiplash Associated Disorders World Congress (Traffic Safety and Auto Engineering Session),* February 1999, Vancouver, BC, pp 361-390.

Koch, M; Kullgren, A; Lie, A; Nygren, A; Tingvall, C. Soft tissue injury of the cervical spine in rear-end and frontal car collisions. *Proceedings of the IRCOBI Conference on Biomechanics of Impacts,* Brunnen, Switzerland, 1995.

Kornhauser, M. Delta-v thresholds for cervical spine injury. SAE Technical Paper Series, 960093, 1-13, 1996.

Krafft, M; Kullgren, A; Lie, A; Tingvall, C. The risk of whiplash injury in the rear seat compared to the front seat in rear impacts. *Traf. Inj. Prev.*, 2003, 4, 136-140.

Krafft, M; Kullgren, A; Lie, A; Tingvall, C. *Assessment of whiplash protection in rear impacts – crash tests and real-life crashes.* Folksam Research, 10660. Stockholm, Sweden, 2004.

Krafft, M; Kullgren, A; Tingvall, C. How crash severity in rear impacts influences short-and long -term consequences to the neck. *Accid. Anal. Prev.,* 2000, 32, 187–195.

Kullgren, A; Krafft, M; Lie, A; Tingvall, C. The effect of whiplash protection systems in real-life crashes and their correlation to consumer crash test programmes. ESV Paper No. 07-0468, 2007.

Kullgren, A; Krafft, M; Nygren, A. Neck injuries in frontal impacts: influence of crash pulse characteristics on injury risk. *Accid. Anal. Prev.,* 2000, 32, 197–205.

Kumar, S; Narayan, Y; Amell, T. Role of awareness in head-neck acceleration in low velocity rear-end impacts. *Accid. Anal. Prev.,* 2000, 32, 233–241.

Lange, JE; Voas, RB. Nightime observations of safety belt use: an evaluation of California's primary law. *AJPH,* 1998, 88(11),1718.

Lamb, SE; Williams, MA; Withers, E; et al. A national survey of clinical practice for the management of whiplash-associated disorders in UK emergency departments. *Emergency Medical Journal,* 2009, 26(9), 644-647.

Langweider, K; Schick, S; Hell, W. Rear-end impact characteristics leading to a dynamic seat test standard proposal. In: Yoganandan N, Pintar FA (eds). *Frontiers in Whiplash Trauma: Clinical and Biomechanical.* The Netherlands: IOS Press; 2000; 467-476.

Lee, WE. Biomechanical analysis and injury causation: an individual-specific and incident-specific approach. *43rd Annual proceedings of the Association for the*

Advancement of Automotive Medicine. September 20-21, 1999, Barcelona, Spain, 438-439.

Linder, A; Avery, M. Change of Velocity and Pulse Characteristics in Rear Impacts: Real World and Vehicle Tests Data. The Motor Insurance Repair and Research Centre. Thatcham, United Kingdom. Available from: http://www-nrd.nhtsa.dot.gov/pdf/nrd-01/esv/esv18/cd/files/18ESV-000285.pdf.

Livingston, M. Whiplash injury: misconceptions and remedies. *Australian Family Physician,* 1992, 21(11), 1642-3–1646-7.

Livingston, M. Whiplash injury and peer copying. *Journal of the Royal Society of Medicine,* 1993, 86, 535–536.

Loeppke, R. The value of health and the power of prevention. *International Journal of Workplace Health Management,* 2009, 1(2), 95-108.

Loeppke, R; Taitel, M; Richling, D; et al. Health and Productivity as a business strategy. *Journal of Occupational and Environmental Medicine,* 2007, 49, 712-721.

Lövsund, P; Nygren, A; Salen, B; Tingvall, C. Neck injuries in rear end collisions among front and rear seat occupants. *International IRCOBI Conference on the Biomechanics of Impacts,* 1988, Bergisch-Gladbach, Germany, 319-325.

Lubin, S; Sehmer, J. Are automobile head restraints used effectively? *Can Fam Physician,* 1993, 39, 1584-1588.

Lundell, B; Jakobsson, L; Alfredsson, B; Jernstrom, C; Isaksson-Hellman, I. *Guidelines for and the Design of a Car Seat Concept for Improved Protection Against Neck Injuries in Rear End Car Impacts*. SAE Paper No. 980301, SAE International Congress and Exposition, Detroit, February 1998.

Mahaffey, T; MacAuley, K; Wright, BA. A study of head restraint use: preliminary findings and implications for a public awareness campaign. *Proceedings of the 32nd Annual Atlantic Schools of Business Conference,* Antigonish, NS, November, 2002.

Maher, J. Report investigating the importance of head restraint positioning in reducing neck injury in rear impact. *Accid. Anal. Prev.,* 2000, 32, 299–305.

Martin, JL; Pérez, K; Marí-Dell'olmo, M; Chiron, M. Whiplash risk estimation based on linked hospital-police road crash data from France and Spain. *Inj Prev,* 2008, 14(3), 185-190.

Martinez, JL; Garcia, DJ. A model for whiplash. *J. Biomech.,* 1968, 1, 23-32.

McConnell, WE; Howard, RP; Guzman, HM; Bomar, JB. Analysis of human test subject kinematic responses to low velocity rear end impacts. In: Vehicle and Occupant Kinematics. SAE: Warrendale PA, 1993, 21-30.

McConnell, WE; Howard, RP; Poppel, JV; Krause, R; Guzman, H; Bomar, JB. Human head and neck kinematics after low velocity rear-end impacts – understanding "whiplash". *Proceedings 39th Stapp Car Crash Conference*, November 8-10, 1995.

McCunney, RJ; Rountree, PP; Barbanel, CS; Borak, JB; Bunn, WB. *A Practical Approach to Occupational and Environmental Medicine*. (3rd Edition). Philadelphia, PA: Lippincott Williams and Wilkins; 2003.

McFadden, M; Powers, J; Brown, W; Walker, M. Vehicle and driver attributes affecting distance from the steering wheel in motor vehicles. *Human Factors,* 2000, 42(4), 676-682.

McNab, I. Acceleration injuries of the cervical spine. *Journal of Bone and Joint Surgery,* 1964, 46, 1797-1799.

Mertz, HJ; Patrick, LM. Investigation of the kinematics and kinetics of whiplash. *Proceedings 11th Stapp Car Crash Conference*, October 10-11, 1967.

Minton, R; Murray, P; Pitcher, M; Galasko, CSB. Causative factors in whiplash injury: implications for current seat and head restraint design. *Proceedings International IRCOBI Conference on the Biomechanics of Impacts,* September 24-6, 1997, Hanover, Germany, pp 207-222.

Minton, R; Murray, P; Stephenson, W. Whiplash injury: Are current head restraints doing their job? *Accid. Anal. Prev.,* 2000, 32, 177–185.

Morris, F. Do head-restraints protect the neck from whiplash injuries? *Archives of Emergency Medicine,* 1989, 6(1), 17-21.

Morris, AP; Thomas, P. Neck injuries in the UK co-operative crash study. SAE 962433, 1996; 476; 317-329.

Motor Insurance Repair Research Centre (Thatcham). 2006. Available from: http://www.thatcham.org/.

Mulhall, KJ; Moloney, M; Burke, TE; Masterson, E. Chronic neck pain following road traffic accidents in an Irish setting and it's relationship to seat belt use and low back pain. *Irish Medical Journal,* 2003, 96(2), 53-54.

Murray, S. Global injury and violence. *Canadian Medical Association Journal,* 2006, 174(5), 620-621.

Murray, CJ; Lopez, AD, editors. *The global burden of disease: a comprehensive assessment of mortality and disability from diseases, injuries and risk factors in 1990 and projected to 2020.* Cambridge (MA): Harvard University Press; 1996.

National Accident Sampling System/Crashworthiness Data System (NASS) 1988-1990. U.S. Dept. of Transportation, National Highway Traffic Safety Administration, 1991.

National Highway Traffic Safety Administration (NHTSA). Head Restraints - Identification of issues relevant to regulation, design, and effectiveness. National Highway Traffic Safety Administration. 1996. Available from: http://www.nhtsa.gov/cars/rules/CrashWorthy/HeadRest/status9/status9.html

NHTSA. Improving the head restraint requirements of Federal Motor Vehicle Safety Standard 202 (Docket No. NHTSA 2000-8570), March 5, 2001.

National Social Marketing Centre (NSMC). United Kingdom. Available from: http://www.nsmcentre.org.uk.

National Tobacco Control Campaign. England, UK. Available from: www.givingupsmoking.co.uk.

Nygren, A. Injuries to car occupants: some aspects of interior safety of cars. A study of five-year material from an insurance company. *Acta Otolaryngologica,* 1984, 395, 1–164.

Nygren, A; Gustafsson, H; Tingvall, C. Effects of different types of headrests in rear-end collisions. *Proceedings 10th International Technical Conference on Experimental Safety Vehicles*, July 1-4, 1985, Oxford, England, pp 85-90.

O'Neill, B. Head restraints – the neglected countermeasure. *Accid. Anal. Prev.,* 2000, 32, 143-150.

O'Neill, B; Haddon, W; Kelley, AB; Sorenson, WW. Automobile head restraints-frequency of neck injury claims in relation to the presence of head restraints. *AJ PH,* 1972, 62, 309-406.

Olsen, O; Middleton, P; Ezzo, J; et al. Quality of Cochrane reviews: assessment of sample from 1998. *BMJ,* 2001, 323, 829–832.

Olsson, I; Bunketorp, O; Carlsson, G; Planath, I; Norin, H; Ysander, L. An in-depth study of neck injuries in rear end collisions. *Proceedings International IRCOBI Conference on the Biomechanics of Impacts,* September 12-14, 1990, Bron, Lyon, pp 269-280.

Ommaya, A; Backaitis, S; Fan, W; Partyka, S. Automotive neck injuries. *Ninth International Technical Conference on Experimental Safety Vehicles,* US Department of Transportation, National Highway Traffic Safety Administration, Kyoto Japan, Nov 1-4, 1982, pp 274-278.

Ono, K; Kaneoka, K; Wittek, A; Kajzer, J. Cervical injury mechanism based on the analysis of human cervical vertebral motion and head-neck-torso kinematics during low speed rear impacts. *Proceedings 41st Stapp Car Crash Conference,* November 13-14, 1997, pp 339-356.

Ono, K; Kanno, M. Influences of the physical parameters on the risk to neck injuries in low impact speed rear-end collisions. *Proceedings International IRCOBI Conference on the Biomechanics of Impacts,* September 8-10, 1993, Einhoven, The Netherlands, pp 201-212.

Ono, K; Kanno, M. Influences of the physical parameters on the risk to neck injuries in low impact speed rear end collisions. *Accid. Anal. Prev.,* 1996, 28(4), 493-499.

Osti, OL; Gun, RT; Abraham, G; Pratt, NL; Eckerwall, G; Nakamura, H. Potential risk factors for prolonged recovery following whiplash injury. *European Spine Journal,* 2005, 14(1), 90-94.

Otremski, I; Marsh, JL; Wilde, BR; McLardy Smith, PD; Newman, RJ. Soft tissue cervical spinal injuries in motor vehicle accidents. *Injury,* 1989, 20(6), 349-351.

Otte, A; Ettlin, TM; Nitzsche, EU. PET and SPECT in whiplash syndrome: a new approach to a forgotten brain? *Journal of Neurology, Neurosurgery and Psychiatry,* 1997, 63, 368-372.

Otte, D; Rether, JR. Risks and mechanisms of injuries to the cervical spine in traffic accidents. *Proceedings International IRCOBI/AAAM Conference on the Biomechanics of Impacts,* 1985, Goetborg, Sweden, pp 17-31.

Parkin, S; MacKay, GM; Cooper, A. How drivers sit in cars. *Accid Anal Prev,* 1995, 27(6), 777-783.

Parmar, HV; Raymakers, R. Neck injuries from rear impact road traffic accidents: prognosis in persons seeking compensation. *Injury,* 1993, 24(2), 75-78.

Pedder, J; Hillebrandt, D. *Head restraint field study: final results.* Rona Kinetics and Associates, Ltd. Report No. RK00-04R.

Prochaska, JO; DiClemente, CC. Stages and processes of self-change of smoking: Toward an integrative model of change. *Journal of Consulting and Clinical Psychology,* 1983, 51, 390-395.

Quinlan, KP; Annest, JL; Myers, B; Ryan, G; Hill, H. Neck strains and sprains among motor vehicle occupants-United States, 2000. *Accid. Anal. Prev.,* 2004, 36(1), 21-27.

Radanov, BP; Sturzenegger, M; Di Stefano, G; Schnidrig, A. Relationship between early somatic, radiological, cognitive and psychosocial findings and outcome during a one-year follow-up in 117 patients suffering from common whiplash. *British Journal of Rheumatology,* 1994, 33, 442-448.

Research Council for Automotive Repairs (RCAR)/ IIWPG Seat-Head Restraint Evaluation Protocol, Version 2.5, 2006.

RCAR. A Procedure for Evaluating Motor Vehicle Head Restraints. Issue 2, February, 2001.

RCAR. IIWPG Protocol for the Dynamic Testing of Motor Vehicle Seats for Neck Injury Prevention. 2004.

Richter, M; Ferrari, R; Otte, D; Kuensebeck, HW; Blauth, M; Krettek, C. Correlation of clinical findings, collision parameters, and psychological factors in the outcome of whiplash associated disorders. *J. Neurol Neurosurg Psychiatry,* 2004, 75(5), 758-764.

Richter, M; Otte, D; Pohlemann, T; Kretteck, C; Blauth, M. Whiplash-type neck distortion in restrained cart drivers: frequency, causes and long term results. *European Spine Journal,* 2000, 9, 109-117.

Roh, LS; Fazzalaro, W. Transection of the trachea due to improper application of automatic seatbelt (submarine effect). *Journal of Forensic Science,* 1993, 38(4), 972-977.

Ruedemann, AD. Automobile safety device-headrest to prevent whiplash injury. *JAMA,* 1957, 24, 164(17), 1889.

Ruedemann, AD. The electroretinogram in degenerative diseases. *International Ophthalmology Clinics,* 1969, 9(4), 1005-1023.

Ryb, GE; Dischinger, PC. Injury severity and outcomes of overweight and obese patients after vehicular trauma: A crash injury research and engineering network (CIREN) study. *The Journal of Trauma: Injury, Infection, and Critical Care,* 2008, 64, 406-411.

Saab, B-R; Usta, J; Hamadeh, G. Head restraint and seat belt use by car drivers in Lebanon. *International Journal of Risk and Safety in Medicine,* 2000, 13, 9-13.

Satoh, S; Naito, S; Konishi, T; et al. An examination of reasons for prolonged treatment in Japanese patients with whiplash injuries. *Journal of Musculoskeletal Pain,* 1997, 5(2), 71-84.

Scaer, RC. *The Body Bears The Burden: Trauma, Dissociation and Disease.* Binghamton, NY: Haworth Medical Press; 2007.

Schmitt, KU; Walz, F; Vetter, D; Muser, M. Whiplash injury: cases with a long period of sick leave need biomechanical assessment. *Eur. Spine J.,* 2003, 12(3), 247-254.

Schneider, LW. *Anthropometry of motor vehicle occupants*. Vol 1-3, University of Michigan Transportation Research Institute UMTRI-83-53/1/2/3, Ann Arbor, MI, 1983.

Scholten-Peeters, GG; Verhagen, AP; Bekkering, GE; et al. Prognostic factors of whiplash-associated disorders: a systematic review of prospective cohort studies. *Pain,* 2003, 104(1-2), 303-322.

Sekizuka, M. Seat designs for whiplash injury lessening. *Proceedings 16th International Technical Conference on the Enhanced Safety of Vehicles,* May 31-June 4, 1998, Windsor, Canada, pp 1570-1578.

Sendur, P; Thibodeau, R; Burge, J; Tencer, A. Parametric analysis of vehicle design influence on the four phases of whiplash motion. *Traf. Inj. Prev.,* 2005, 6(3), 258-266.

Severy, DM; Brink, HM; Baird, JD. Backrest and head restraint design for rear-end collision protection. SAE No. 680079, 1968.

Severy, DM; Mathewson, JH; Bechtol, CO. Controlled automobile rear-end collisions. An investigation of related engineering and medical phenomena. *Canadian Services Medical Journal,* 1955, 727-759.

Siegmund, GP; Heinrichs, BE; Wheeler, JB. The influence of head restraint and occupant factors on peak head/neck kinematics in low-speed rear-end collisions. *Accid. Anal. Prev.,* 1999, 31(4), 393-407.

Soltermann, B. Cranio-cervical acceleration/deceleration trauma in Switzerland: Documentation on initial consultation – incapacity to work – prevention. *Proceedings Cervical Spine Injuries in Road Traffic Accidents Conference,* November 5-6, 2007, Munich, Germany.

Spitzer, W; Skovron, ML; Salmi, LR; Cassidy, JD; Suissa, S; Zeiss, E. Scientific monograph of the Quebec task force on whiplash-associated disorder; Redefining "Whiplash" and its management. *Spine Supplement,* 1995, 20(8), S1-S73.

States, JD; Balcerak, JC. The effectiveness of head restraints in rear end impacts. Report no. DOT-HS-800-877. 1973. Washington DC: US Department of Transportation.

States, JD; Balcerak, JC; Williams, JS; et al. Injury frequency and head restraint effectiveness in rear end impact accidents. *Proceedings of the 16th Stapp Car Crash Conference,* 1972, Detroit, MI, pp 228-257.

States, JD; Balcerak, JC; Williams, JS; et al. Injury frequency and head restraint effectiveness in rear-end impact accidents. *Proceedings of the 16th Stapp Car Crash Conference. Society of Automotive Engineers,* 1973, New York, NY, pp 228–257.

Sterner, Y; Gerdle, B. Acute and chronic whiplash disorders - A review. *Journal of Rehabilitation Medicine,* 2004, 36(5), 193-210.

Subzwari, S; Desapriya, E; Scime, G; Babul, S; Jivani, K; Pike, I. Effectiveness of cataract surgery in reducing driving-related difficulties: a systematic review and meta-analysis. *Inj. Prev.,* 2008, 14(5), 324-328.

Svensson, MY; Aldman, B; Hansson, HA; et al. Pressure effects in the spinal canal during whiplash extension motion: a possible cause of injury to the cervical spinal ganglia. *Proceedings International IRCOBI Conference on the Biomechanics of Impacts*, September 8-10, 1993, Einhoven, The Netherlands, pp 189-200.

Szabo, TJ. Influence of seat properties on occupant kinematics and injury potential in low-speed rear impacts. In: Yoganandan N, Pintar FA (eds).

Frontiers in Whiplash Trauma: Clinical and Biomechanical. The Netherlands: IOS Press; 2000; 348-405.

Szabo, TJ; Voss, DP; Welcher, JB. Influence of seat foam and geometrical properties on biorid p3 kinematic response to rear impacts. *Traf. Inj. Prev.,* 2003, 4(4), 315-323.

Szabo, TJ; Welcher, JB. Human subject kinematics and electromyographic activity during low speed rear impacts. *Proceedings 40th Stapp Car Crash Conference,* 1996, Albuquerque, NM.

Szabo, TJ; Welcher, JB; Anderson, RD; et al. Human occupant kinematic response to low speed rear impacts. *Proceedings 38th Stapp Car Crash Conference,* October 31 – November 4, 1994, Paper 921573.

Taylor, JA; Burke, J; Gavencak, J; Panwar, P. Knowledge and application of correct car seat head restraint usage among chiropractic college interns: a cross-sectional study. *Journal of the Canadian Chiropractic Association,* 2005, 45, 32-39.

Teifke, A; Degreif, J; Geist, M; Schild, H; Strunk, H; Schunk, K. Der Sicherheitsgurt: Auswirkungen auf das Verletzungsmuster von Autoinsassin. *Rof Fortschr Geb Rontgenstr Neuren Bildgeb Verfahr*, 1993, 159, 278-283.

Temming, J; Zobel, R. Frequency and risk of cervical spine distortion injuries in passenger car accidents; significance of human factors data. *Proceedings of the 1998 International IRCOBI Conference on the Biomechanics of Impacts*, 1998, Bron, France, pp 219-233.

van den Kroonenberg, A; Philippens, H; Cappon, J; Wismans, J; Hell, W; Langweider, K. Human head-neck response during low-speed rear end impacts. *Proceedings of the 42nd Stapp Car Crash Conference,* 1998, SAE 983157, pp 207-221.

van der Velde, G; van Tulder, M; Cote, P; Hogg-Johnson, S; Aker, P; Cassidy, JD; Members of the Scientific Secretariat of The Bone and Joint Decade 2000-2010 Task Force on Neck Pain and Its Associated Disorders. The sensitivity of review results to methods used to appraise and incorporate trial quality into data synthesis. *Spine,* 2007, 32(7), 796-806.

Vasavada, AN; Danaraj, J; Siegmund, GP. Head and neck anthropometry, vertebral geometry and neck strength in height-matched men and women. *J. Biomechanics,* 2008, 41, 114-121.

Verhagen, AP; Karels, C; Bierma-Zeinstra, SMA; et al. Ergonomic and physiotherapeutic interventions for treating work-related complaints of the arm, neck or shoulder in adults. A Cochrane Systematic Review. *Europa Medicophysica,* 2007a, 43(3), 391-405.

Verhagen, AP; Scholten-Peeters, G; van Wijngaarden, S; et al. Conservative treatments for whiplash. *Cochrane Database Syst Rev,* 2007b, 2, CD003338.

Versteegen, GJ; Kingma, J; Meijler, WJ; ten Duis, HJ. Neck sprain in patients injured in car accidents: a retrospective study covering the period 1970-1994. *Eur Spine J,* 1998, 7, 195-200.

Viano, DC. *Role of the Seat in Rear Crash Safety.* Warrendale, PA: Society of Automotive Engineers. (2002).

Viano, DC. Seat properties affecting neck responses in rear crashes: A reason why whiplash has increased. *Traf. Inj. Prev.,* 2003a, 4(3), 214–227.

Viano, DC. Seat influences on female neck responses in rear crashes: A reason why women have higher whiplash rates. *Traf Inj Prev,* 2003b, 4(3), 228–239.

Viano, DC. Seat design principles to reduce neck injuries in rear impacts. *Traf. Inj. Prev.,* 2008, 9, 552-560.

Viano, DC; Gargan, MF. Headrest position during normal driving: implications to neck injury risks in rear crashes. *39th Annual Proceedings of AAAM Conference.* October 1995, Chicago, IL.

Viano, DC; Gargan, MF. Headrest position during normal driving: implication to neck injury risk in rear crashes. *Accid. Anal. Prev.,* 1996, 28(6), 665-674.

Viano, DC; Olsen, S. The effectiveness of active head restraint in preventing whiplash. *J. Trauma,* 2001, 51(5), 959-969.

Watanabe, Y; Ichikawa, H; Kayama, O; Ono, K; Kaneoka, K; Inami, S. Relationship between occupant motion and seat characteristics in low-speed rear impacts. SAE No. 1999-01-0635, Occupant Protection (SP-1432), pp 13-22.

Welcher, JB; Szabo, TJ. Relationships between seat properties and human subject kinematics in rear impact tests. *Accid. Anal. Prev.,* 2001, 33(3), 289-304.

Welcher, JB; Szabo, TJ. Relationship between seat properties and human subject kinematics in rear impact tests. *Proceedings WAD Compendium/Auto Safety and Auto Engineering,* Vancouver, BC, 1999, pp 243-274.

West, D; Gough, J; Harper, G. Low speed rear-end collision testing using human subjects. *Accident Reconstruction Journal,* 1993, 5(3), 22-26.

White, MI; Davis, D; Holland, JH; Green, LW; Liang, MH. Using conferences as strategic events to support knowledge mobilization. *Proceedings of the World Congress on Neck Pain,* January 20-22, 2008, Los Angeles, California, pp 134.

Wiklund, K; Larsson, H. Saab active head restraint (SAHR) – seat design to reduce the risk of neck injuries in rear impacts. SAE Technical Paper Series 980297. Warrendale, PA: Society of Automotive Engineers, 1998, pp 1-7.

Wood, DP. Safety and the car size effect: a fundamental explanation. *Accid. Anal. Prev.,* 1997, 29(2), 139-151.

Yoganandan, N; Pintar, FA; Kleinberger, M. Cervical spine vertebral and facet joint kinematics under whiplash. *Journal of Biomechanical Engineering,* 1998, 120, 305-307.

Yoganandan, N; Pintar, FA; Kleinberger, M. Whiplash injury biomechanical experimentation. *Spine,* 1999, 24, 83-85.

Young, AL; Ragel, BT; Su, E; Mann, CN; Frank, EH. Assessing automobile head restraint positioning in Portland, Oregon. *Inj. Prev.,* 2005, 11(2), 97-101.

Zhu, S; Layde, PM; Guse, CE; et al. Obesity and risk for death due to motor vehicle crashes. *AJPH,* 2006, 96(4), 734-739.

Zuby, DS; Lund, AK. Minor neck injuries in rear crashes – international problem and progress. *Proceedings of the Neck Injuries in Road Traffic and Prevention Strategies*. 2007, Germany.

INDEX

A

Abbreviated Injury Scale, xiv
accidents, 58, 69, 72, 76, 78, 80
accounting, xii
activation, 1, 6, 8
adjustment, vii, viii, ix, x, xv, xvi, xix, xx, 9, 25, 27, 29, 31, 38, 43, 51, 52
adults, 47, 81
advertisements, 58
advertising, 53, 57, 58
age, ix, 7, 14, 15, 16, 17, 47, 54, 71
alcohol, 52, 57
anatomy, 16
anxiety, xv
assessment, 22, 45, 46, 50, 65, 76, 77, 79
attitudes, 44, 53, 55, 58, 59
Australia, xv, 14, 23, 58, 66, 70
Austria, 73
availability, 22, 51
avoidance, 44, 48
awareness, viii, x, 1, 25, 27, 28, 30, 39, 47, 49, 52, 53, 54, 56, 57, 58, 74

B

back pain, 47, 58, 67, 76
barriers, 55
behavior, 22, 44, 52, 53, 54, 55, 56, 57, 61
beliefs, 55, 58, 59, 66, 67
benchmarking, 10
bending, 5
beneficial effect, 6
bias, 41
biomechanics, 9, 44
BMI, 14
body mass index, 14
brain, 47, 78

C

cadaver, 68
campaigns, 52, 54, 59
Canada, xiv, xvii, 12, 25, 26, 27, 28, 29, 30, 33, 34, 38, 47, 49, 50, 58, 68, 79
candidates, 45
capsule, 9
car accidents, 66, 67, 81, 82
caregivers, 42
cataract, 80
causation, 72, 74
channels, 56
children, 57
classification, xi, 45, 47
clinical assessment, 47
clinical judgment, 42
closure, 22
codes, 47
coding, 45, 47
cohort, 47, 67, 68, 79
collaboration, 42, 46, 49, 58

commercials, 59
communication, 53, 56
community, 42, 43, 44, 51, 52, 57
compatibility, 11, 20, 71
compensation, 16, 21, 22, 46, 47, 67, 78
competition, 55
complex interactions, 21
complexity, 61
components, xvii, 2
composition, 41
compression, xiii, 2, 6
computer simulations, 1, 2
concussion, 47
Congress, 49, 61, 65, 66, 69, 71, 72, 74, 75, 82
consensus, xi, 35
consumers, 55
consumption, 56, 66
control, 9, 15, 17, 22, 46, 56
correlation, 4, 19, 71, 74
cost-benefit analysis, 43, 72
costs, xiv, xv, xvii, 36, 43, 44, 47, 48, 58
counsel, 29
covering, 82
cross-sectional study, 27, 59, 81
culture, 70

D

data analysis, 28
database, 45, 46, 65
deaths, 68, 73
decisions, 42
deduction, 42
definition, xii
deformation, 9, 20
delivery, 48
demographic data, 56
demographics, 15
developed countries, 22
developing countries, 23
direct costs, 48
disability, viii, x, xiii, xiv, 21, 23, 25, 43, 46, 48, 49, 50, 51, 67, 76
discomfort, xiv
disorder, 47, 80
displacement, xvi, 6, 8, 9
distortions, xi
divergence, xi
doctors, 29, 45
draft, 34
duration, 4, 67

E

ears, xx, 26
economics, 47
Education, 52, 53
employees, 48
energy, vii, xii, 3, 4, 6, 7, 8, 10, 14, 19, 20, 34, 37
energy transfer, xii
England, 56, 77
environment, 46
environmental factors, xiii
epidemic, 69
epidemiology, 23, 44, 46
ergonomics, 44, 46
EU, 78
Euro, 36, 38, 69
Europe, xiii, 12, 25, 33, 34, 38
evolution, vii, x, 39, 61
exercise, 42
expertise, 41, 54

F

fabrication, 36
failure, 42
family, 29, 51
fat, 14
fears, 55
females, xiii, 11, 15, 16, 27, 28
focus groups, 55
France, 17, 19, 67, 70, 73, 75, 81
furniture, 47

G

General Motors, 4, 8
general practitioner, 58
generation, 7
Germany, 65, 66, 68, 71, 75, 76, 80, 83
goals, 53
government, 27, 49, 50
gravity, xix, 7, 34
groups, 14, 45, 52, 55
guidelines, xi, 7, 25, 33, 43, 46, 47, 50, 59

H

hands, 11
harmonization, 34, 36
hazards, 44, 46
headache, xii, 14
health, xvii, 14, 26, 29, 44, 45, 46, 47, 48, 50, 51, 53, 54, 56, 58, 66, 75
health care, 14, 26, 44, 47, 51
health care system, 47
health education, 53
health insurance, 66
health services, 45
height, xvi, xix, xx, 3, 4, 6, 15, 33, 34, 35, 37, 81
heterogeneity, 41
hip, 34, 36
human resources, 42
human subjects, 8, 11, 67, 82
hypothesis, 2, 14, 15, 68

I

identification, 46
impairments, viii, x, xiii
implementation, xix, 59, 61
incentives, 22, 55, 56
incidence, xiii, xv, xviii, xix, xx, 9, 14, 15, 21, 22, 47
inclusion, 45
incompatibility, 20
individual differences, 15
industry, 36, 44, 45
infrastructure, 23, 51
injury claims, xvii, 10, 45, 48, 65, 77
innovation, xvii, 7
insight, 55, 57
instructors, 29
insurance, xiii, xiv, xvii, 21, 22, 26, 29, 36, 39, 44, 45, 46, 65, 67, 77
interaction, 20, 71
internal validity, 42
intervention, xvii, 22, 52, 58, 67
investment, 42, 58, 59
Ireland, 68
Italy, 70

J

Japan, xv, 12, 23, 68, 71, 77
joints, 66
jurisdiction, 22, 52

K

kinetics, 76
Korea, 30, 71

L

law enforcement, 51, 52
leadership, 46
Lebanon, 29, 79
legislation, 61, 65
leisure, 48
light trucks, 27
likelihood, 9, 17, 59
limitation, xi
linkage, 8
links, 44
litigation, 70
lying, 66

M

males, xx, 11, 15, 16, 28, 30

management, 46, 51, 53, 58, 65, 66, 70, 74, 80
mandates, xvi
mandible, 71
manipulation, 43
manual systems, x
market, 7, 54, 58
marketing, viii, x, 31, 51, 52, 53, 54, 55, 56, 57, 59, 61, 70
mass media, 58, 66
matrix, 38
measurement, 35
measures, 20, 42, 54
media, 31, 52, 53, 58
medical care, xv, 48
men, xix, xx, 7, 15, 16, 26, 29, 45, 81
messages, 52, 53, 56, 58, 59
meta-analysis, 65, 70, 80
misconceptions, 75
modeling, 50
models, xviii, 3, 8, 27, 36, 46
momentum, 14
morphology, xvi
mortality, ix, 76
motion, xii, xiii, xiv, 1, 2, 3, 5, 6, 8, 9, 21, 28, 35, 43, 77, 79, 80, 82
motivation, 39, 52
movement, vii, xi, xii, xvii, xviii, 56, 70
muscle mass, 15
muscle strain, 2
muscles, 1, 4, 16, 19

N

National Institute for Occupational Safety and Health, 49
neck injury, viii, x, xviii, xix, 7, 9, 10, 14, 15, 18, 22, 37, 42, 44, 48, 66, 69, 72, 73, 74, 75, 77, 82
neglect, 45
nerve, 19
Netherlands, 35, 66, 67, 68, 73, 74, 77, 80, 81
network, 29, 79
neuroscience, 44
New England, 67
New South Wales, xiv
New Zealand, 23
North America, xiii, xx, 23, 47
Norway, 58
nurses, 46

O

obesity, 14
observations, 74
occupational health, viii, x, 46, 47, 50
operator, 50
overweight, 79

P

pain, xi, xii, xiii, xiv, xvii, xix, 2, 3, 4, 5, 14, 16, 19, 22, 30, 39, 43, 46, 47, 48, 49, 50, 58, 59, 61, 65, 66, 67, 71, 76
parameter, 35
parents, 57
passive, 9, 41
pathology, xii
pathways, 45
pedal, 16
pelvis, 8
percentile, xix, 10, 11, 15, 35
permit, xvi
personal benefit, 53
pessimism, 59
PET, 78
planning, 59, 63
plausibility, 44
police, 27, 45, 52, 61, 75
pollution, 49
poor, x, xx, 10, 21, 26, 27, 38, 45, 52
population, xiii, xv, 8, 15, 22, 25, 27, 28, 36, 48, 51, 52, 53, 58, 59, 61, 66, 67, 71
positive relation, 22
positive relationship, 22
posture, 7, 16, 65
power, xix, 75
preparedness, 1
pressure, 2, 8, 10, 19, 36
prevention, vii, viii, x, 22, 23, 36, 43, 46, 47, 48, 50, 51, 53, 58, 61, 68, 69, 72, 75, 80

productivity, 46, 48
prognosis, 5, 78
program, 49, 55
protective factors, 17
protocol, 34, 35, 65
public awareness, xiii, 31, 75
public health, xvii, 22, 43, 46, 61, 70
public sector, 53
public service, 27
pulse, 5, 18, 74

Q

quality of life, xv, xvii

R

range, xiii, 3, 42, 43
ratings, 9, 10, 11, 33, 36, 37, 38, 39, 49, 50, 61, 69, 72
recognition, xvii, 1, 26
recovery, 14, 20, 22, 43, 45, 51, 59, 78
regulation, 33, 34, 35, 36, 61, 77
regulations, xx, 33, 34, 35, 36, 39, 68
relationship, 1, 4, 11, 46, 61, 76
relevance, xi, 66
reliability, 38, 42
repair, 49
research funding, 49
resistance, 18
resources, 36, 50, 51, 53
retention, vii, 8, 34
risk factors, vii, ix, 12, 13, 14, 21, 22, 23, 43, 44, 52, 76, 78
Royal Society, 75

S

safety, ix, x, xiv, xv, xix, 1, 21, 26, 27, 28, 29, 30, 34, 36, 37, 39, 43, 44, 45, 46, 50, 51, 52, 54, 58, 67, 68, 69, 74, 77, 79
sample, xix, 23, 28, 29, 30, 42, 57, 77
satisfaction, xv
school, 51
search, 48
seat belt use, 76, 79
sensitivity, 81
sensors, 1, 9
September 11, 68
SES, 54
severity, ix, xi, xiii, 3, 7, 19, 20, 23, 53, 69, 74, 79
sex, xix, 15, 16, 54
sex differences, xix, 16
shape, xiv, 2, 6, 9
shaping, 50
shear, xiii, 2, 6, 9, 16, 37, 68
shear deformation, 9
simulation, 2, 44
smoking, 78
social change, 56
societal cost, x, xiv, xvii
software, 2, 9
Spain, 17, 19, 75
speed, xiv, xviii, 1, 2, 3, 8, 10, 18, 19, 20, 21, 27, 37, 38, 56, 67, 68, 70, 73, 77, 78, 80, 81, 82
spine, xi, xii, xiv, 2, 3, 5, 7, 14, 16, 17, 18, 35, 66, 68, 70, 71, 72, 74, 76, 78, 81, 83
sports, 58, 68
sprain, 66, 67, 82
sprains, 69, 78
stages, xiii, 2, 54, 68
stakeholders, 50
standards, xx, 1, 27, 33, 36, 39, 45
static geometry, vii, 37, 38
statistics, 18, 56
strain, vii, 3, 9, 19
strategies, vii, viii, x, 23, 42, 43, 50, 51, 52, 54, 57, 66
strength, 9, 15, 34, 81
stress, 4, 16
stretching, xiv, 2
students, 29
Sun, 74
Sweden, 19, 28, 58, 67, 71, 73, 74, 78
Switzerland, 74, 80
symptoms, xi, xii, 7, 19, 41, 66
syndrome, 78

synthesis, xi, xiii, 14, 19, 22, 41, 42, 81

T

target population, 53, 56
team members, 29
television advertisements, 58
tension, xiii, 2, 4, 9, 37
test procedure, 11
thinking, 54
threat, xiv
threshold, 4, 18
tin, xii
tissue, xii, xix, xx, 4, 14, 18, 47, 66, 71, 74, 78
tobacco, 56
torsion, 73
total energy, 21
Toyota, 6, 8
trachea, 79
traffic, ix, xi, xii, xiii, xiv, 13, 14, 15, 19, 23, 29, 43, 44, 51, 52, 67, 68, 69, 71, 76, 78
training, 46, 49, 52
trajectory, 9
translation, 7, 53
transport, 51
trauma, 29, 66, 70, 79, 80
trial, 81

U

uncertainty, 17
uniform, 18
United Kingdom, xiv, 75, 77
United Nations, 34
United States, 78
universities, 49
updating, 50

V

vacuum, 53
validation, 5, 67
validity, 42
values, 52
variability, 35
variables, 11
variation, 27
vehicles, vii, ix, x, xv, xvi, xviii, xix, 7, 11, 17, 20, 21, 25, 26, 28, 29, 30, 33, 34, 36, 39, 45, 48, 51, 52, 56, 61, 68, 76
velocity, xii, 5, 19, 20, 38, 74, 75, 76
vertebrae, xvi, 10, 16, 65
victims, 71
violence, 76
vulnerability, 15, 16, 45

W

wealth, 42
women, xix, xx, 7, 15, 16, 26, 28, 29, 30, 43, 44, 81, 82
work absenteeism, 47
workers, xiii, 46, 47, 48, 58, 67, 69
working population, 47
workplace, xvii, 46, 48